G000127386

100
GREATS

SALFORD
RUGBY LEAGUE CLUB

Five Salford players, all featured in this book, line up for Great Britain before the First Test against New Zealand at Carlow Park, Auckland in August 1936. From left to right: Gus Risman (captain), Emlyn Jenkins, Barney Hudson, Billy Watkins, Alan Edwards.

The Welsh XIII for the match against France, played at Toulouse in March 1959. For three of the Salford 100 'Greats'– John Cheshire, Graham Jones and Dai Moses (then with Swinton) – it was the only Rugby League representative honour of their careers. From left to right, back row: John Thornley (Halifax), Don Vines (Wakefield Trinity), Malcolm Davies (Bradford Northern), Rees Thomas (Wigan), Cheshire, Charlie Winslade (Oldham), Gordon Lewis (Leigh), George Parsons (Salford), Moses. Front row: Garfield Owen (Halifax), Tommy Harris (Hull), Lionel Emmett (Blackpool Borough), Jones.

100 GREATS

SALFORD
RUGBY LEAGUE CLUB

WRITTEN BY
GRAHAM MORRIS

TEMPUS

First published 2001
Copyright © Graham Morris, 2001

Tempus Publishing Limited
The Mill, Brimscombe Port,
Stroud, Gloucestershire, GL5 2QG

ISBN 0 7524 2196 4

Typesetting and origination by
Tempus Publishing Limited
Printed in Great Britain by
Midway Colour Print, Wiltshire

Cover illustrations:

Front cover: Steve Blakeley looks for runners as he sets up another attacking play. Apart from a brief spell at Warrington, he is the longest-serving member of the current Salford City Reds squad, having originally joined the club in November 1992.

Back cover: Three true 'greats' of the Salford club – all of them having achieved the ultimate honour of being Great Britain tour captains (from top to bottom): Jimmy Lomas (captain of the first British tourists in 1910); Gus Risman (who led the so-called 'Indomitables' of 1946); Chris Hesketh (skipper of the 1974 squad that included six Salford players).

Other rugby titles from Tempus Publishing:

0 7524 1896 3	Bradford Bulls Rugby League Club	Robert Gate	£9.99
0 7524 1895 5	Castleford Rugby League Club	David Smart	£9.99
0 7524 1831 9	Halifax Rugby League Club	Andrew Hardcastle	£9.99
0 7524 1822 X	Headingley Rugby Voices	Phil Caplan	£9.99
0 7524 2190 5	Hull Rugby League Club Voices	Raymond Fletcher	£10.99
0 7524 1641 3	Hunslet Rugby League Club	Les Hoole	£9.99
0 7524 1140 3	Leeds Rugby League Club	Phil Caplan and Les Hoole	£9.99
0 7524 1897 1	Salford Rugby League Club	Graham Morris	£9.99
0 7524 1830 0	Sheffield Eagles Rugby League Club	John Cornwell	£9.99
0 7524 1883 1	St Helens Rugby League Club	Alex Service	£9.99
0 7524 1870 X	Warrington Rugby League Club	Eddie Fuller and Gary Slater	£9.99
0 7524 1881 5	Yorkshire Rugby League	Les Hoole	£9.99
0 7524 2069 0	The Barbarians Story	Alan Evans	£16.99
0 7524 2181 6	Cardiff RFC 1945-2000	Duncan Gardiner and Alan Evans	£10.99
0 7524 1851 3	The Five Nations Story (hb)	David Hands	£19.99
0 7524 1570 0	Newport RFC 1950-2000	Steve Lewis	£9.99

PREFACE

An invitation from Tempus Publishing to bring together a volume containing one hundred of the greatest players ever to pull on the famous red jersey of the Salford City Reds Rugby League Club was a challenge that was simply too good to resist. I quickly realised, however, that 'challenge' was the operative word! As with any established sports club, it is very easy to reel off the first dozen names or so, and no true historian of the Salford club could ever take issue with the inclusion of star names such as Jimmy Lomas, Gus Risman or David Watkins. If you were to dig a little deeper, then every supporter of this eminent club will have their own particular heroes. We need only to consider that ever-popular pastime of selecting a team of all-time favourites to realise that no two individuals will ever arrive at the same result!

My approach was to take the comparatively easy option and include every player who, from the formation of the club in 1873, had taken part in at least 200 matches. After all, if you were picked so many times you would have to be a 'good 'un'. That accounted for 70 players – only 30 to go. Easy? Think again! Try selecting 30 players from a list of almost 1,300 to have represented Salford down the years. The fact that I had, inevitably, to leave out so many notable names of the past – and present – serves as a testimony to the quality of those contained in the final list.

Many of the players included in this book are true 'Greats' – international stars who have graced the game at the very highest level. Others, perhaps less gifted, have earned their place through their commitment and loyalty to the Salford club over the many seasons that they played. Amongst the wonderfully talented players that I have had to exclude are those who established their reputations either before or after being with the Reds. Bill Burgess, Garry Jack and Martin Offiah are prime examples – all superstars who, sadly from the Salford fans' point of view, achieved most of their accolades elsewhere. On the opposite side of the coin, I felt it was right to include rising stars Malcolm Alker and Gary Broadbent. Both are in the early stage of their careers but each, surely, is destined for a place in the Salford 'Hall of Fame' in the years ahead.

Before closing, I would like to say a heartfelt 'thank you' to David Watkins – one of the greatest of the 'Greats' – for so readily agreeing to write the foreword to this book.

Graham Morris
Worsley
July 2001

FOOTNOTE

In my previous compilation for Tempus Publishing, *Images of Sport – Salford Rugby League Club*, I included a photograph of Salford from 1887/88 with the comment that it was 'The earliest known team photograph'. After that book went to press, the historian's nightmare occurred, although it was a happy one, when a much older photograph, taken in 1881/82, came into my possession. I am pleased to have the opportunity to include this historically important picture – the only one I have seen showing Salford in their original hooped jerseys – on page 49 of this book.

ACKNOWLEDGEMENTS

With a publication that contains so many photographs and statistics, there is a list of people to offer a sincere thank you to. Over the years the following individuals, some no longer with us, have been particularly supportive in helping collect the material that is featured in this volume: Timothy Auty, Tony Collins, Trevor Delaney, Robert Gate, Andrew Hardcastle, Percy Harrison, Julie Hollis, Bert Hughes, John Jenkins, Michael Latham, Stephen Owen (William Eagles Limited), John Riding, Ron Robinson, Irvin Saxton, Alan Shaw, Brian Snape and Tom Webb. Thanks also to the players both past and present – featured in this work – who willingly allowed me to pick their brains. I am especially grateful to Peter Jackson for providing several of the contemporary photographs, including the front cover picture of Steve Blakeley.

I have referred to many newspapers and periodicals to aid my research. In particular, I would like to credit the excellent reporting of Jack McNamara, my all-time favourite Rugby League scribe, who covered the sport over many years for the *Manchester Evening News*, and Tom Bergin – alias 'Ajax' – who wrote on the affairs of the Salford club for over half a century in the *Salford City Reporter*. James Higson's 1892 book *The History of the Salford Football Club* and the autobiographies of Gus Risman (*Rugby Renegade*, 1958) and David Watkins (*The David Watkins Story*, 1971 and *David Watkins: An Autobiography*, 1980), have all proved wonderful sources of reference. My thanks also for the valued help of the following organisations: the *Advertiser & Salford City Reporter*, the *Rugby Leaguer*, League Publications Limited, Colourplan Design and, as always, the helpful staff at the Salford Local History Library.

I have made all reasonable effort to trace copyright holders for photographs that I have used, although it has been difficult to locate the original source in many cases. My appreciation too, to the Salford City Reds personnel, in particular chief executive, David Tarry, commercial manager, Ray Hill, club secretary, Christine James and media manager, Carolyn Derbyshire, for their help and enthusiastic support.

STATISTICAL NOTE

The career summary for each player included in this volume relates to appearances for Salford only and covers the following:

1873-1896. All matches played by the club during the Rugby Union period. These are predominantly 'friendly' meetings but do include Lancashire Club Championship fixtures (1892 to 1896). Due to the vagaries of the point scoring systems during this time, 'points' totals for players who made their debut before the 1891/92 season are not given.

1896-2001. All official fixtures played by the club, since joining the Northern Union (Rugby Football League from 1922) in April 1896. Substitute appearances, introduced in 1964, are included.

1915-1918. Friendly 'wartime' matches played at the time of the First World War. There was no official fixture list, but a full programme of unofficial games took place.

'Representative honours' are for a player's complete career and cover international and county appearances in Rugby League and Rugby Union, but exclude achievements at school and junior level. 'Club honours' are for a player's complete career in senior Rugby League and are assumed to be for Salford except where indicated in brackets.

All the statistics are up to and including 29 July 2001.

All players recruited by Salford from the 1896/97 season are assumed to be signed from other senior Rugby League clubs, except where the following abbreviations appear:

ARL – Amateur Rugby League Club

RU – Rugby Union Club

FOREWORD

by David Watkins, MBE

The date 19 October 1967 was the start of one of the most enjoyable periods of my life. It was my introduction to The Willows, home of Salford Rugby League Club. My time at Salford was certainly not a bed of roses, as coping with a big signing-on fee and the tough, hard, uncompromising game of Rugby League was not an easy task. The game of Rugby League prides itself on its no nonsense approach, but its skills delight its supporters. It is also the envy of many Rugby Union diehards because of its basic rules and the players' commitment, which added together, makes the game a wonderful spectacle. It has also given me great friends and memories that will live with me forever.

Many people in my native Wales thought of my signing as a quick way of making money before retirement. The resentment of my signing for a large fee, by the press and some of Rugby League's greats, was expressed verbally and in print but, at the end of it all, I felt I overcame it to have a most enjoyable time and a big opportunity to play the hardest game in the world – there was no hiding place!

The Salford club was greatly admired, but it was also jealously hated, and it was certainly discussed throughout rugby circles and beyond. The man who made all this possible was a man whom I respected more than any other in rugby, G.B. (Brian) Snape, whose vision to re-establish the Reds to their former glories was most imaginative. He was responsible for putting me in touch with so many of the Reds greats. These heroes include Gus Risman, Hugh Duffy, Dai Moses, Billy Watkins, Barney Hudson, Emlyn Jenkins, Billy Williams and Les Bettinson. Their advice, guidance, support and, indeed, friendship made my early years at the club the better for knowing them, as did two opposites in the coaching stakes: Griff Jenkins and Cliff Evans – what a contrast, but both so influential.

As always when asked, special mention must be made of some players, the likes of Colin Dixon, Paul Charlton, Chris Hesketh, Maurice Richards, Mike Coulman, Steve Nash, Ken Gill, Eric Prescott, Keith Fielding – world class! But, then again, it was a team game and the following were special: Peter Smethurst, Doug Davies, Charlie Bott, Terry Ogden, Stuart Whitehead, Aiden Breen, Trevor Rabbit, Graham MacKay, Peter Walker, and one who was my mentor, Jackie Brennan – what a player!

My welcome at The Willows was unforgettable, and this remained with me throughout my time at the club. To be in the same team as so many great players was a privilege. If only the game had not divided into Union and League, these players would have had universal applause. It was such an honour for me to play, captain, and perform in front of The Willows faithful – it was simply fantastic. I have so much respect for the fans and the players, the likes of whom I will never ever forget. The Rugby League still has a good future. I believe both codes should continue to operate separately. They have both produced marvellous players. If only the League boys had had equal exposure.

To Graham Morris, I thank you for honouring 100 Salford greats.

David Watkins
Newport
June 2001

100 SALFORD GREATS

Malcolm Alker
Jack Anderton
Peter Banner
Alf Barrett
Les Bettinson
Steve Blakeley
Ian Blease
Charlie Bott
Syd Boyd
Joe Bradbury
Jackie Brennan
Gary Broadbent
Jack Brown
R. (Bob) Brown
W. (Billy) Brown
Andy Burgess
Jimmy Burgess
Aubrey Casewell
Paul Charlton
John Cheshire
Walter Clegg
Mike Coulman
Harry Council
Tom Craven
George Curran
George Currie
Ephraim Curzon
W. (Paddy) Dalton
Tom Danby
Dai Davies
Eifion (Jack) Davies
H.C. (Bert) Day
Colin Dixon
Hugh Duffy

Harry Eagles
Alan Edwards
Jack Feetham
Keith Fielding
Albert Gear
Ken Gill
Arthur Gregory
Alan Grice
E.C. (Teddy) Haines
Tommy Harrison
Bryn Hartley
George Heath
Chris Hesketh MBE
Barney Hudson
James Jackson
Emlyn Jenkins
Dai John
Graham Jones
James Jones
Brian Keavney
Tom Kent
Steve Kerry
Tom King
Harry Launce
Mark Lee
Jimmy Lomas
Tom McKinney
David Major
William Manwaring
Reg Meek
Bernard Mesley
Alf Middleton
Frank Miles
Sammy Miller

Dai Moses
Jack Muir
Steve Nash
Harold Osbaldestin
Eric Prescott
Dave Preston
Dai Rees
Jack Rhapps
Maurice Richards
A.J.F. (Gus) Risman
Jack Roberts
Steve Rule
Joe Shaw
Peter Smethurst
Dan Smith
Fergie Southward
Evan Thomas
Harold Thomas
Willie Thomas
Pat Tunney
Silas Warwick
David Watkins MBE
W. (Billy) Watkins
Stuart Whitehead
Jack Williams
Peter Williams
Sam Williams
Stewart Williams
Syd Williams
Tom Williams
W.A. (Billy) Williams
Ernie Woods

The twenty who appear here in italics are each covered on two pages instead of the usual one.

Malcolm Alker
Hooker, 1997- present

Birthplace: Wigan
Signed from: Wigan St Partick's ARL

Debut: 25 August 1997 v. Sheffield Eagles (away)

Appearances: 93 (includes 1 as substitute)
Tries: 24
Goals: 0
Points: 96

Representative honours: none
Club honours: none

Malcolm Alker signed for the Salford Reds in May 1997 from the famous Wigan amateur club St Patrick's when he was nineteen years old. He played first for the Orrell St James' club before joining the team that his father, also Malcolm, had turned out for some twenty years earlier.

The move to St Patrick's brought him under the coaching wing of former Reds favourite, Gerard Byrne. Surprisingly, Alker did not win any representative honours at amateur level. 'It was strange really' he said, 'I was surrounded by quality players and I always seemed to get overlooked'. Nonetheless, Byrne recognised the potential in Alker. 'I am not certain, but I believe it was him that told Andy Gregory about me. He came down to watch me and that's how I came to play at Salford.' Salford coach Gregory had also been a colleague of his father's in his time at St Patrick's.

It was not very long before Alker, a determined, hard-working hooker and a demon tackler, was impressing the Salford coaching staff and chasing a first-team place. In August 1997, he stood in for resident number nine, New Zealander Peter Edwards, in two matches whilst Edwards himself relocated to cover the full-back position in the absence of Gary Broadbent. His breakthrough came midway through the 1998 season, when recalled to the team for the match at Halifax on 14 June. Since then he has established himself as the number one choice. In the 2000 season, when still only twenty-one, he had the ultimate honour of leading his Salford colleagues for two matches during June and July, in the absence of regular captain Darren Brown. 'I felt a sense of achievement to be in charge. It was a real honour to have the trust of the coaches and players to do that', he commented.

When the squads were announced for the 2000 World Cup tournament, there was real anticipation in the Salford camp that he would be in the England squad. Although nominated, it was not to be. 'I was disappointed because I thought it was one of my best chances, with Keiron Cunningham playing for Wales and Terry Newton out injured' he said. It cannot be too long, however, before Alker does earn his first representative call and joins the list of true Salford greats.

Jack Anderton

Wing three-quarter, 1887-1889

Birthplace: Wigan
Signed from: Wigan

Debut: 17 September 1887 v. Rochdale Hornets (home)
Final match: 22 April 1889 v. Barrow (away)

Appearances: 52
Tries: 17
Goals: 25

Representative honours: Tourist (RU) 1888, Lancashire RU
Club honours: none

Jack Anderton was Salford's first outstanding wingman, a fact recognised by his invitation to take part in the inaugural tour of Australia and New Zealand in 1888. The first player recruited from Wigan by Salford, he was to make a significant impact in just two seasons at the club.

Although not a spectacular winger, he was effective, employing a direct running style and – even in those early years – he had perfected the art of vigorously handing off any opponent that barred his route. He scored a try and a goal in only his second outing at Bradford, helping his new club to an unexpected victory over the Yorkshire giants and contributing a hat-trick of goals towards a big win at Broughton Rangers during October. That first season saw him top the club try chart with 11 touchdowns and goal list with 17 – in a period when goal success was more modest.

His exploits gained the attention of the Lancashire county committee and in November 1887 he represented East Lancashire against West Lancashire in the county trial match at Whalley Range. In that instance, it did not lead to selection for Lancashire but the end of season pioneering

visit to Australasia more than compensated. In New Zealand, the press quickly became aware of his prowess. After the opening match – an 8-3 win over Otago at Dunedin, on 28 April – one scribe noted: 'Anderton, the left wing, was the most prominent back in the British team, being strong and fast with an effective fend and difficult to stop.' Anderton's second half try, a strong touchline run into the corner, had turned the game in the tourists' favour after Otago had led at the break.

His second season with Salford saw him gain recognition for the county against Cumberland at Warrington on 28 February 1889, his only appearance for Lancashire. The following month he lined up for Salford in the prestigious game against the New Zealand Maori side, the first rugby tourists to Britain. In the concluding match of 1888/89, he scored a goal in the victory at Barrow, but this was to be his final appearance for Salford. He resigned, unexpectedly, on the eve of the 1889/90 season, whereupon he returned to Wigan. He featured in the county trial match at Whalley Range in November 1889 but failed to impress the selectors.

Peter Banner

Scrum-half, 1968-1975

Birthplace: Rochdale
Signed from: Spotland Rangers ARL (Rochdale)

Debut: 18 October 1968 v. Rochdale Hornets (home)
Final match: 31 March 1975 v. Wigan (home)

Appearances: 180 (includes 9 as substitute)
Tries: 24
Goals: 1
Points: 74

Representative honours: Wales, Wales World Cup Squad 1975, Lancashire
Club honours: Rugby League Championship 1973/74, Lancashire Cup 1972, Yorkshire Cup 1976 (Leeds), BBC2 Floodlit Cup 1974/75

Signed from Rochdale amateurs Spotland Rangers in March 1967, Peter Banner was an unlikely star in the costly Salford outfit of the 1970s. Although small, he was a gutsy performer. A resounding victory over Huddersfield, in September 1971, sent Jack McNamara, of the *Manchester Evening News*, into poetic mood as he wrote: 'Little Peter Banner, a pygmy amongst giants, is rapidly winning a special place in the affections of Salford fans. They wince when he is tossed about like a rag doll by big ugly forwards and cheer when, seemingly indestructible, he bounces back. Banner was at his perky best in last night's 37-4 destruction of Huddersfield at The Willows. He rode his pack like a gnat on an elephant, nipping under tackles on solo breaks and linking up cleverly with his support.'

His breakthrough came against Hull on 12 February 1971 when, after impressing in the reserves with half-back partner Ken Gill, the duo were given a first-team chance. It was a turning point, and Banner became a prominent figure in the successes that followed. This included the 1973/74 championship, the 1972 Lancashire Cup final victory over Swinton – scoring a try in

Salford's first major trophy win since 1939 – and the BBC2 Floodlit Cup triumph of 1974/75. He also played in three losing finals: the Lancashire Cup of 1973 and 1974 and the Players Trophy in 1973.

Representative honours came in 1972, for Lancashire against Cumberland and Yorkshire. Banner qualified, courtesy of his Newport-born grandfather, to appear for Wales on 16 February 1975, the first of eight outings for the Principality that also cemented his place in the Welsh World Cup squad to Australasia in 1975.

The arrival of Steve Nash in August 1975 cost him his first-team place, although this did not go down well with the fans at the time, Banner being a firm favourite. After a month on loan at Halifax, he transferred to Featherstone Rovers for £4,500 in September 1975, ironically to replace Nash. In 1976, he moved to Leeds in a £5,000 deal and, after sharing in their 1976 Yorkshire Cup final success over Featherstone, he helped them to the 1977 Challenge Cup final. Despite having played in every round, he surprised everyone by emigrating to Australia and missed the Wembley trip.

Alf Barrett

Centre three-quarter, 1888-1895

Birthplace: Ringley, near Prestwich
Signed from: Ringley

Debut: 27 October 1888 v. Broughton Rangers (home)
Final match: 30 April 1895 v. Oldham (home)

Appearances: 223
Tries: 47
Goals: 9

Representative honours: Lancashire RU
Club honours: Rugby League Championship 1901/02 (Broughton Rangers), Lancashire RU Club Championship 1892/93, Lancashire League Championship 1896/97 (Broughton Rangers) and 1898/99 (Broughton Rangers)

Centre three-quarter Alfred Barrett proved to be one of Salford's most consistent players during the Rugby Union era. He was virtually always present and only missed twelve games during his seven seasons at the club, five of them due to playing for Lancashire. He commenced playing rugby with his village side in Ringley in 1886, when he was sixteen. He performed well enough to catch the attention of Swinton, who offered him a one-month trial in their reserves. In the event, he only took part in two mid-week games during that period and left feeling frustrated. Hearing Salford was on the lookout for centres, he sent a letter to the honorary-secretary James Higson requesting a trial. Higson responded by asking Barrett how well he could play. 'Well, I got two tries on Saturday for Ringley' was the reported response.

Although still only eighteen, he made his first team debut for Salford in the game with their local rivals, Broughton Rangers, on 27 October 1888. The following week, he showed what he was capable of when he dropped a goal to win the match for his new club at Liverpool Old Boys. In that first season with Salford, he played against the touring New Zealand Maori side and by the conclusion of the 1888/89 campaign, Higson

was pleased to write: 'During the season he played exceedingly well for us, considering his youth and inexperience of first-class matches.' In spite of missing the opening six fixtures, he still managed to take part in 33 games for his new club, registering 6 tries and 2 goals.

Barrett's wing partner for most of the 223 matches that he played for Salford was speedster Frank Miles, and the pair built up a formidable reputation. Although only 5 ft 4 in tall, Barrett was an elusive and quick player, and eagerly provided scoring chances for the deadly finishing of Miles. He also proved his skill when it came to scoring goals in broken play, recording seven drop-goals amongst the nine that he put over the bar for Salford. He went on to captain Salford for two seasons and was a reserve for the annual North of England versus South match.

The 1892/93 season was a particularly memorable one for Barrett. To begin with, he was a member of the first Salford team to win a trophy, the inaugural Lancashire Club Championship, playing in all fifteen of the Reds' title-chasing games. The other significant event was his debut for Lancashire against Cumberland on 19 November at Whalley Range, going on to make a further three appearances for the county during that season. In the season of 1893/94, he

Alf Barrett with the Lancashire team before the Roses match against Yorkshire at Bradford, on 25 November 1893. From left to right, back row: W. McCutcheon (Oldham), G. Woodward (Tyldesley), H. Case (Swinton), J.C. Gould (Liverpool Old Boys). Middle row: A.M. Crook (secretary), T. Foulkes (St Helens), W. Unsworth (Wigan), J. Simpson (Rochdale Hornets), James Bate (Warrington, at back), S. Lees (Oldham), R.P. Wilson (Liverpool Old Boys). Front row: A. Ashworth (Rochdale Hornets, standing), Barrett, J. Valentine (Swinton), J. Jolley (Warrington), John Bate (Warrington).

was virtually an ever present in the Lancashire team, playing in six of the fixtures – although surprisingly he was not selected again.

In August 1895, most of the north's senior clubs resigned from the English Rugby Football Union to create what was, in effect, the forerunner of the Rugby League. The key issue had been the refusal by the RFU to agree to broken time payments by the northern clubs, to compensate their essentially working-class players for missing Saturday shifts. Salford, for another season at least, would remain with the RFU, but for Barrett, that would be one season too many, and he transferred his loyalty to Broughton Rangers who had elected to join the rebels. It was difficult to blame him as, during the 1894/95 season – his last with Salford – he had played in only seventeen matches due to the club being suspended for ten weeks by the Lancashire county committee on the grounds of alleged professionalism.

For Barrett, it was a good move, sharing in the

Rangers' Lancashire League Championship success of 1896/97, a feat they repeated in the 1898/99 season. In 1901/02, he played his part as they claimed the new Northern Rugby League Championship, set up to replace the previously separate Lancashire and Yorkshire county leagues. An historic 'double' was complete when they overpowered Salford 25-0 in the Challenge Cup final at Rochdale, although Barrett missed that match due to injury.

Having represented Lancashire under Rugby Union rules, he was hopeful of gaining selection in the new set up. Barrett appeared in two trial matches for the county: the first at Wheaters Field in October 1897 and another one year later at Warrington. In both cases, he did not persuade the selectors and it signalled the end of his county aspirations. Barrett continued to give good service to Broughton Rangers until the end of the 1902/03 season, returning to Salford as a guest player for a friendly with Barton on 28 April 1897.

Les Bettinson

Centre three-quarter, 1957-1969

Birthplace: Millom
Signed from: Millom RU

Debut: 9 March 1957 v. Batley (home)
Final match: 10 September 1969 v. Wigan (home)

Appearances: 319 (includes 2 as substitute)
Tries: 75
Goals: 10
Points: 245

Representative honours: Cumberland
Club honours: none

It is doubtful if anyone filled more roles than Leslie James Bettinson did at The Willows, before his lengthy association with the club finally concluded in 1991, at which point he stepped down from the board after thirty-four years with the club. As a player, he was the classic centre: upright and ever alert, he possessed a graceful running style and an elegant sidestep. He was first spotted by Gus Risman in 1952, at a time when Risman was in charge at Workington Town. Bettinson recalled: 'He saw me playing Rugby League for Millom when I was seventeen and I had a trial with Workington's reserve team, ironically against Salford. Another trialist on the wing was Ike Southward'. Southward, of course, later became one of the all-time great Cumbrian wingers and was twice the subject of record transfer fees for the game.

In those days, however, young men still had to fulfil their National Service commitment and, as Bettinson's was about to commence, he elected not to sign. Afterwards, he returned to rugby, but this time to play for the Millom Rugby Union club, which he combined with playing for the Leeds Teacher Training College RU team, where he was studying. 'I was over eighteen and I could not risk a ban by playing Rugby League, as I was a reserve for the Cumberland Rugby Union county side'.

Risman then reappeared on the scene but was now the club coach at Salford. 'He asked me when my next match was and, by coincidence, the Training College team was playing in Castleford the same day as Salford. After the match, he invited me to join the Salford party for a meal. The next week I went to The Willows to play in a trial for Salford in a first team game against Batley and I was signed after the match.'

Bettinson was, unfortunately, not likely to win many trophies with Salford as a player at that time, although he did manage a few personal highlights. One of these was that, from August 1962 until August 1964, he never missed a match for Salford, an amazing sequence of 81 consecutive games. Then in 1966/67, his Testimonial season, he was the club's top try scorer with 11. 'We were not a leading club in my playing days, but my favourite memory was our run in the 1967 Rugby League Challenge Cup, when we put out the previous finalists St Helens and Wigan on their own grounds. We drew 5-5 with St Helens at Salford in the first round and that was a shock in itself. When Tom van Vollenhoven scored an early try in the replay, we were expected to lose heavily, but hung on to be only 3-0 down at half time. In the second half, I remember ducking under a tackle and scoring. A few minutes later I did a cross kick which hit the side of the St Helens post and, in the scramble, our wing Paul Murphy followed up to score. We won 8-3. It was unbelievable! Then we went to Wigan and won 18-6 and I scored again.' He also scored at Dewsbury in the third round, but the dream ended with an unexpected 9-7 defeat.

Although club honours evaded him, he still achieved individual recognition. On 11 September 1957, he made his first appearance for Cumberland, just six months after signing for Salford, the opposition being Yorkshire at Hull's Boulevard ground. That match was lost, but Bettinson soon tasted victory with the county just five days later when Lancashire was defeated 22-12 at Workington. Altogether, he was to represent Cumberland seven times during the next ten seasons, the most memorable being in 1965/66 and 1966/67, when he shared in two county championship successes.

Bettinson retired as a player in September 1969 and was invited to stay on at the club to support coach Griff Jenkins with the training sessions. When Cliff Evans took over from Jenkins in May 1970, Bettinson's role continued and he took on the title of assistant coach. 'I was delighted when I was asked to help with the training. I could not see myself retiring from the game – it is the main core of my life' he said. When Evans reluctantly retired through poor health midway through the 1973/74 season, Bettinson took over the reigns as senior coach. It was the beginning of one of the most successful periods of his career, as he led the Reds to two championship successes in 1973/74 and 1975/76, and victory in the 1974/75 BBC2 Floodlit Cup final. Under his charge, the team also reached the 1976 Premiership Trophy final and the Lancashire Cup finals of 1974 and 1975. 'When we won the championship in 1974 and again in 1976 I felt really proud. It is a long hard bash from August to April and to do it twice represented years of commitment and hard work. I never wanted any of the glory – that

One of Les Bettinson's fondest memories – the shock 18-6 Challenge Cup victory at Wigan in February 1967. Here he watches over a Wigan opponent, supported by Bob Burdell (left) and Joe Southward.

was for the players. I was always happy to be sixteenth man'.

When he resigned as coach in March 1977, he was offered a place on the board. He accepted and became the club representative on the Rugby League management committee. In February 1985, more recognition came his way when he took over as the Great Britain manager, leading his country on the tour of Australia and New Zealand in 1988 with Malcolm Reilly as coach. His ultimate achievement came when elected as the first president of the Rugby Football League for 1988/89. He was also the chairman of the Rugby League coaching committee and is the author of two books; *The Rugby League Coach* (1986) and *In the Lions' Den* (1991).

Steve Blakeley

Stand-off half, 1992-1999, 2000- present

Birthplace: Leigh
Signed from: Wigan

Debut: 22 November 1992 v. Wigan (home)

Appearances: 214 (includes 8 as substitute)
Tries: 66
Goals: 672
Points: 1600

Representative honours: England
Club honours: First Division Championship 1996, Centenary First Division Championship 1995/96, Divisional Premiership 1996

At the commencement of the 2001 season, Steve Blakeley stood shoulder-to-shoulder with some of the greatest marksmen in the history of the Salford club. His prolific goal scoring had placed him third in the all-time list, with only David Watkins and Gus Risman lying ahead. A further target was reached in the 32-24 victory at Huddersfield on 17 June 2001, when his try and five goals enabled him to leapfrog Jimmy Lomas and move into third slot (also behind Watkins and Risman) on the club's list of top point-scorers.

An elusive and quick-thinking stand-off, Blakeley commenced his rugby career with Leigh Rangers amateur club, having played for England and Lancashire schoolboys through various age levels. He signed for Salford in November 1992 aged twenty, the first match being against his former club, Wigan, for whom he had played eight times as a substitute. In his first season, he competed with another ex-Wigan half-back in Wayne Reid for the stand-off berth before establishing himself as the regular choice. He kicked his first century of goals (106) in 1996 and followed that with 101 the next season – the club's first SuperLeague campaign.

Apart from the Reds winning the Centenary First Division Championship of 1995/96, his most memorable term was the first summer season of 1996 when he skippered the Reds to a First Division and Premiership double. In the same year, he made his international debut, representing England against France and Wales in the European SuperLeague championship. In July of 1998, injury forced him to forgo the honour of being captain to the Emerging England team against Wales at Widnes, although he did play for England a third time, against France at Hull's Boulevard in October 1999.

At the conclusion of the 1999 season, he transferred to Warrington but, after the opening months of the 2000 season, returned to The Willows. His comeback match was on 7 May at home to Halifax. 'I felt a bit frustrated at Warrington' he said. 'I was not getting any games. I was playing here and there but at twenty-seven, as I was then, I need to be playing every week'. The next milestone for Blakeley will be to top the club's goal and point charts in 2001 for the ninth successive season, thereby equalling Lomas' long standing record set in 1910.

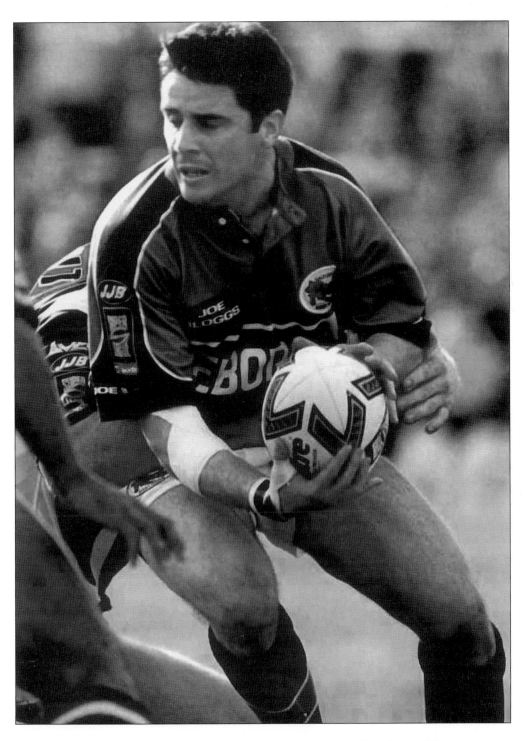

Steve Blakeley in classic pose, looking to off-load the ball in the tackle.

Ian Blease
Second row forward/prop forward, 1985-1997

Birthplace: Swinton
Signed from: Folly Lane (Swinton) ARL

Debut: 31 March 1985 substitute v. Bramley (home)
Final match: 18 April 1997 substitute v. London Broncos (away)

Appearances: 252 (includes 36 as substitute)
Tries: 49
Goals: 0
Points: 196

Representative honours: Lancashire
Club honours: Second Division Championship 1990/91, First Division Championship 1996, Second Division Premiership 1991, Divisional Premiership 1996

In 1990/91, Ian Blease became the first Salford captain since 1976 to lead his team to trophy success, giving chairman John Wilkinson his most rewarding campaign since taking the helm in 1982. Blease was only twenty years old when he joined Salford on 11 March 1985, making a quick debut at substitute in the 48-14 win over Bramley later that month. His first full appearance was on 14 April 1985 at home to Runcorn Highfield, playing in the second row and scoring a try. Blease developed into a tough tackling, aggressive forward – a real handful for the opposition – but he was also an inspiring leader, taking over as skipper in 1990.

In October 1988, he appeared in his first final, as substitute for the concussed Peter Williams, when the Reds contested the destination of the Lancashire Cup against Wigan, losing 22-17. At the end of the 1989/90 season, Salford were relegated from the top division but, under team manager Kevin Tamati and captain Blease, the Reds bounced back impressively. The first signs of a revival appeared early in the new season when Salford fought their way through to the Lancashire Cup final in September 1990 and came close to upsetting a strong Widnes side.

Salford eventually lost 24-18 after giving the Chemics a fright, Blease leading by example and scoring a well-taken try. It was in the Second Division Championship that Salford really set the pace. With only one defeat, he ended the chase by lifting the championship bowl, followed by more glory at Old Trafford when Halifax were defeated in the Premiership final 27-20.

His success with the team rubbed off and he appeared in the Lancashire side on 18 September 1991 in the 'War of the Roses' match at Headingley, his only representative honour. During the mid-1990s, Blease struggled with injury problems and, apart from a substitute appearance, missed the clubs Centenary First Division success in 1995/96. He made amends by playing his part in winning the 1996 First Division – the first summer season – thereby assisting promotion to the new SuperLeague. At the climax to that season in September, he played at prop in the Divisional Premiership final when Keighley Cougers were beaten 19-6. He made just one substitute appearance the following season and in January 1998, he joined Swinton.

Charlie Bott
Prop forward, 1967-1971

Birthplace: Thorne, near Doncaster
Signed from: Oldham

Debut: 19 August 1967 v. Wigan (away)
Final match: 25 April 1971 v. Halifax (home)

Appearances: 160 (includes 1 as substitute)
Tries: 12
Goals: 1
Points: 38

Representative honours: Great Britain
Club honours: Second Division Championship 1963/64 (Oldham)

Charlie Bott was the type of prop forward that every successful side needs. A big, dominating forward, he was always in the thick of things, leading by example and tackling anything that moved – provided it was wearing a rival jersey!

He began by playing Rugby Union in his native Doncaster for Old Thornesians. In 1962, he signed for Oldham, sharing in their magnificent 1963/64 revival season which saw the club promoted as Second Division champions and get agonising close to their first Wembley trip, when they lost in a second replay to Hull Kingston Rovers. Bott's outstanding displays attracted the attention of the international selectors in 1966, and he won a cap for Great Britain against France on 5 March. Regrettably, Britain put on a poor show, losing 8-4 at Wigan's Central Park and he was to be one of the casualties of that performance, not gaining selection for his country again.

During the 1967 close season, he moved to Salford with a transfer fee of £4,000 changing hands. It was at the start of Brian Snape's ambitious plan to build a team worthy of the city. Bott's first appearance in the red jersey, shared with another newcomer, Chris Hesketh, was in a pre-season charity match at Wakefield on 11 August 1967, the Reds winning 29-6.

Bott's biggest occasion in the Salford colours was at the 1969 Challenge Cup final at Wembley. Following the semi-final victory over Warrington, he addressed the supporters at the Variety Centre that evening, telling them proudly: 'I have waited ten years for this!' A voice quickly retorted 'Yes, but we've waited thirty Charlie!' He was to miss out on further big days with Salford when he decided to emigrate to Australia following the 1970/71 season. In what would be his final home match, against Halifax in a championship play-off on 25 April, he was captain for the day. Salford won comfortably 33-3, and Bott kicked his only goal for Salford when club captain David Watkins relinquished, in the sixty-seventh minute, what would have been his 150th goal of the season, in converting a Ken Gill try. That turned out to be Bott's final match as suspension, after being sent off in a stormy match against Rochdale a month earlier, ruled him out of the following round of the play-off, which Salford lost at Leeds.

Syd Boyd

Wing three-quarter/centre three-quarter, 1923-1933

Birthplace: Wigan
Signed from: Wigan

Debut: 29 September 1923 v. Wakefield Trinity (away)
Final match: 13 December 1933 v. London Highfield (away)

Appearances: 299
Tries: 56
Goals: 0
Points: 168

Representative honours: none
Club honours: Rugby League Championship 1932/33, Lancashire Cup 1931, Lancashire League Championship 1932/33

Sydney Boyd was another Wigan lad who left his hometown club to seek fortune elsewhere. Emerging through the local junior ranks, he made his Wigan debut in April 1921 playing centre at Batley in virtually a reserve side, the star performers being rested for an upcoming Championship semi-final. Over the next two seasons, he played a further 21 matches but could not rely on his place. His final appearance was his biggest for the club – a Challenge Cup semi-final against Hull on 14 April 1923. Played at Huddersfield, Wigan lost 13-9.

Salford signed Boyd at the onset of the 1923/24 campaign. Times were bad at The Willows, the club having been on a slippery slope since the Championship win of 1914. Alf Beecroft, who covered the club's affairs in the *Salford City Reporter*, later reflected: 'The club had no spare cash to splash around on star recruits. And it was quite a venture when they bought Boyd, a winger who had had long service with Wigan and he did the Reds quite a power of good at the time'. Boyd excelled in Salford's team, his tackling noted to be 'as good as any three-quarter in the league' and he was a regular until the end of the 1932/33 season. His first five seasons were not very

rewarding, the highlight being the match against the New Zealanders in November 1926, which was lost 18-10.

The arrival of Lance Todd as coach in 1928 changed everything and, although Boyd had been playing professionally for over seven years when Todd arrived, he was still only twenty-seven. Under Todd, he took part in Salford's first Lancashire Cup final appearance in 1929. Although defeated 15-2 by Warrington at Wigan, Boyd must have enjoyed being in the limelight at last. His biggest disappointment was missing the 1931 Lancashire Cup final, failing a morning fitness Test to an ankle injury (received in the semi-final with Barrow) but he played a full part in winning the cup, appearing in all the previous rounds. He also contributed to the winning of the Rugby League Championship – although not appearing in the final – and Lancashire League Championship in 1932/33. His last match for the Reds came in 1933/34 at London's White City Stadium against London Highfield, his only appearance that season.

Joe Bradbury

Hooker/prop forward, 1930-1940

Birthplace: Wigan
Signed from: Wigan district ARL

Debut: 11 January 1930 v. Australian Touring Team (home)
Final match: 12 October 1940 v. Wigan (home)

Appearances: 299
Tries: 15
Goals: 0
Points: 45

Representative honours: none
Club honours: Rugby League Championship 1932/33, 1936/37 and 1938/39, Rugby League Challenge Cup 1945 (Huddersfield), Lancashire Challenge Cup 1931, 1934, 1935 and 1936, Lancashire League Championship 1932/33, 1933/34, 1934/35, 1936/37 and 1938/39

James (Joe) Bradbury was a fierce, hard tackling forward. A fiery character, he helped build the platform upon which Lance Todd's talented back division of the 1930s could perform. Signed as a hooker from the Wigan amateur ranks, he had a tough opening match against the Australian tourists in his only appearance of the 1929/30 season, replacing the regular rake Fred Shaw. After several isolated first-team outings, he was allocated a regular place in the team from April 1931. From the 1931/32 season, the industrious Bradbury earned his corn at prop forward, competition for the hooking role having intensified with new signing Bert Day joining Shaw as a contender.

Bradbury did not receive any representative honours, although many thought he should have played for Lancashire. His consolation was to help Salford dominate the club scene throughout the 1930s. He took part in four Rugby League Championship finals, sharing the successes of 1932/33, 1936/37 and 1938/39 and the bitterness of defeat in 1933/34. Sadly for Bradbury, he missed out on the biggest day of all when Salford defeated Barrow at Wembley in 1938, being named as a reserve for

the match – so near and yet so far! He partially made up for this by playing at the Twin Towers the following year against Halifax, but came away as a loser. He appeared in all five Lancashire Cup finals contested by Salford during the decade, adding four winners medals in the process, and scoring a rare try in the 1935 victory over Wigan.

The arrival of the Second World War meant he was destined to play his last game for Salford in 1940, when the club suspended activities until peace returned. Bradbury, along with others, sought his rugby as a guest with other clubs. In 1944/45 he turned out for Huddersfield 18 times and had a place in their Challenge Cup final team against Bradford, taking part in all the rounds and the first leg of a two-legged final. Huddersfield won 13-9 on aggregate, and Bradbury was finally able to add that elusive Challenge Cup winner's medal to his collection. He obviously impressed the Fartowners and signed permanently in October 1945. He played a further 25 times, the most important of which was the Championship final of 1946, when they finished runners-up to Wigan.

Jackie Brennan
Stand-off half/scrum-half, 1959-1970

Birthplace: Wigan
Signed from: Blackpool Borough

Debut: 19 August 1959 v. Whitehaven (home)
Final match: 20 October 1970 substitute v. Widnes (home)

Appearances: 329 (includes 12 as substitute)
Tries: 70
Goals: 3
Points: 216

Representative honours: Lancashire
Club honours: none

In 1967, Alan Prescott, writing in the *Manchester Evening News* said: 'Jackie Brennan would usually be high up the list of my footballers of the season for his sheer consistency and cleverness but, after watching him guide Salford to victory in the second round cup-tie at Wigan, I was even more impressed by his skill. Brennan played out of his skin. He has been an outstanding player for years, content to do his job for his clubs, Blackpool Borough and Salford, and never seeming bothered about being passed over for higher honours.' Those words came from the former Great Britain captain, after witnessing Salford's shock 18-6 win at Wigan in the 1967 Challenge Cup run, having already disposed of St Helens in the opening round. Prescott was just one of many fellow professionals to heap praise on his shoulders over the years.

Brennan arrived at The Willows from Blackpool Borough for £5,000 in August 1959. While with Borough he had received glowing reports, after signing from Wigan junior rugby in 1954. He was picked for Lancashire twice in 1958, playing at stand-off, his partner in both matches being a teenage Alex Murphy. Surprisingly, during his time at Salford, Brennan never regained his county place.

In his first season with Salford, he played at stand-off partnered by the veteran scrum-half Billy Banks, although, for the final match, he found himself reunited with Terry Dunn who had also transferred from Blackpool. His partnership with Dunn continued until September 1963, following which, Brennan found he was repositioned to scrum-half where he became the acknowledged 'brains' behind the team. It was in this position that he was to play at Wembley in 1969, partnered by David Watkins, who had that season taken over the captaincy from Brennan. It was Brennan who carefully guided Watkins through his debut in September 1967. Watkins said later: 'The steadying presence of Jackie Brennan proved invaluable'.

In his last few seasons at Salford he played at loose forward, a position he occupied in his last full appearance at Huddersfield on 4 October 1970. After deservedly receiving a £3,500 testimonial cheque in 1970, he joined Warrington on a free transfer, saying on his departure: 'I am grateful for all Salford have done for me. They gave me a wonderful benefit and the supporters have always given me a fair hearing.'

Gary Broadbent

Full-back, 1997-present

Birthplace: Barrow
Signed from: Widnes

Debut: 6 April 1997 v. Halifax Blue Sox (away)

Appearances: 123
Tries: 25
Goals: 0
Points: 100

Representative honours: Great Britain Academy Tourist 1996, Great Britain Academy, Emerging England
Club honours: none

Gary Broadbent has developed into one of the bravest and most reliable full-backs to play for Salford, following his transfer from Widnes Vikings in April 1997 for £50,000. An outstanding schoolboy prospect, he had progressed through the various age levels for both Lancashire and England, and joined the Walney Central amateur club in Barrow. Widnes was alerted to his potential, moving in quickly to sign him up in March 1993 when he was seventeen years old. 'Dennis McHugh was the coach of England schoolboys and on the staff at Widnes, which is how they knew about me' explains Broadbent.

He spent four years at Widnes, making his first-team debut for them during the 1994/95 season and playing in 60 matches. Eventually, though, he requested a transfer. 'I was still working in Barrow and travelling down to Widnes for training and playing. Salford had just gone into the SuperLeague and offered me a full-time contract which I jumped at.'

Whilst at Widnes he had had his first taste of post-school international Rugby League when picked for the Great Britain Academy international against France in 1996. Even better was his selection for the seven-match Academy tour to New Zealand that same year

and he played in all three Tests against the Junior Kiwis. The tour party was captained by Salford's Nathan McAvoy and included another Red – Ian Watson – in the squad. 'It was a good experience to go over there and learn. A lot of the players from the tour had gone on to make big names but, after returning from New Zealand, I felt dejected when no SuperLeague club came in for me at first. I was grateful to Salford coach Andy Gregory for giving me the opportunity.'

Since making his first appearance in Salford colours during April 1997, he has gone from strength to strength, establishing himself as one of the most popular players at the club. To date, his biggest disappointment has to be the Challenge Cup semi-final defeat by Sheffield Eagles in March 1998 when the Twin Towers of Wembley seemed to be on the horizon. Later that year, in July, he played for the Emerging England team against Wales at Widnes. He was nominated for a place in the England 2000 World Cup squad and, although overlooked on that occasion, he is knocking on the international door.

Jack Brown
Prop forward/second row forward, 1945-1951

Birthplace: Salford
Signed from: Pendlebury Juniors ARL

Debut: 1 September 1945 v. Warrington (away)
Final match: 20 October 1951 v. Batley (away)

Appearances: 218
Tries: 21
Goals: 12
Points: 87

Representative honours: Lancashire
Club honours: Rugby League Challenge Cup 1953 (Huddersfield), Yorkshire Cup 1952 (Huddersfield)

Jack Brown – nicknamed 'Bomber' by the fans – was still a teenager when he joined Salford in September 1938. His signature was the outcome from several trial matches during the previous month with the reserves, but it was seven long years before he finally made his senior debut. This took place at Warrington in Salford's second match after the restoration of peacetime rugby following the Second World War, when he appeared in the second row. A week later, he recorded the first of his 21 tries for the Reds in a 17-5 home victory over Hull. During that first campaign he also kicked 12 goals when Gus Risman – in what would turn out be his last season at Salford – was unavailable.

Most of Brown's 218 appearances came in the back row of the pack, although he did turn out at prop forward 46 times, most of those being in his first two seasons at the club. He was recognised as being a tough, uncompromising forward, and often found himself in trouble with the referee! In those early post-war years, Salford struggled to recapture the form of the 1930s and there were few highlights, although he did play for the Reds in their 13-2 defeat against the 1948 Australian tourists on 2 October. On 3 May 1949, he was awarded his only representative honour when he played in the second row for Lancashire against Yorkshire at Halifax, sharing in a 12-3 victory.

Brown played his last match for Salford at Batley in October 1951, registering his final try for the club in a 17-11 loss. His £1,000 transfer to Huddersfield in November 1951 turned out to be a rewarding one for Brown personally. It would provide him with two winner's medals, the only ones of his career, and both of those came in the 1952/53 season. The first was in the Yorkshire Cup final at Headingley when Batley were defeated 18-8 in November. The second – and most prized – came at Wembley in April, when favourites St Helens were conquered 15-10 in a physical encounter. Sharing the glory with him in the pack that day was ex-Salford colleague George Curran. In September 1954, having played 87 times for Huddersfield, he transferred to Belle Vue Rangers. Fate decreed it would be the last season for that club and Brown played in their finale at Workington Town on 5 May 1955, after appearing in 28 matches for the Manchester outfit.

R. (Bob) Brown

Wing three-quarter/centre three-quarter, 1932-1938

Birthplace: Wigan
Signed from: Wigan

Debut: 12 March 1932 v. Hull Kingston Rovers (home)
Final match: 10 December 1938 v. Rochdale Hornets (away)

Appearances: 251
Tries: 136
Goals: 0
Points: 408

Representative honours: Lancashire
Club honours: Rugby League Championship 1932/33 and 1936/37, Rugby League Challenge Cup 1938, Lancashire Cup 1934, 1935 and 1936, Lancashire League Championship 1932/33, 1933/34, 1934/35 and 1936/37

Robert (Bob) Brown not only dazzled on the pitch, but off it as well! Gus Risman, years later, recalled – 'The crowd loved Bob as a player, and they loved him as a character. He was the best dressed man in Rugby League. He would turn up at the ground, sartorially elegant in a polo jumper, plus fours, but no stockings, and wearing slip-on sandals! His wife was just as pleasing a character. She would arrive at the ground with Bob and she nearly always carried with her a marmoset. That marmoset became a Salford fan too!'

He commenced his professional career with Wigan after starting out with the local Platt Lane amateur club, joining Salford in 1932. He was to share in many successes over the next few years including two Championships, in 1932/33 and 1936/37 (although he missed the final in the latter case), and the 1938 Wembley victory. In 1933/34, he had a phenomenal season on the wing, when his 45 tries eclipsed the twenty-seven-year-old record of 34, set by Jimmy Lomas. In the process, he also established a milestone, scoring tries in nine consecutive matches from January until March, equalled in 1996 by Nathan McAvoy.

The arrival of Alan Edwards in 1935 saw him employed more as a centre, where he was just as adept. When he gained the first of nine Lancashire county caps in 1932, one journalist noted 'Brown has, at last, received recognition of his abilities by his selection for the county. For a long time he has been one of the most consistent three-quarters in the Rugby League without any reward coming his way. He is equally as good a centre as a wing, and there is no fear concerning him justifying his selection'.

In a match against Wigan in 1937, he fractured a rib early in the game but played on, making a try and scoring one himself. During the second half he was rushed to hospital in intense pain. 'I felt all right at first but just before the interval it got really bad. I came on again in order that we should not be too short handed. I am glad that we won!' he said later. During August 1939, he moved to Rochdale Hornets, the club he last played against for Salford. He turned out 25 times for the Hornets in 1939/40, but the arrival of the Second World War effectively ended his career.

W. (Billy) Brown

Forward, 1895-1908, 1918

Birthplace: Salford
Signed from: unknown

Debut: 28 December 1895 v. St Helens Recs (away)
Final match: 9 February 1918 (wartime match) v. Broughton Rangers (home)

Appearances: 278 (includes 1 in wartime)
Tries: 13
Goals: 29
Points: 97

Representative honours: none
Club honours: none

William 'Billy' Brown had probably the most amazing story of any Salford forward, his twenty-two years encompassing the Rugby Union era and the First World War. After an inauspicious start at St Helens Recs, in a game abandoned through heavy rain, he played in Salford's final match under Rugby Union jurisdiction at Broughton in April 1896, in only his sixth appearance. He was also involved in the Reds' first Northern Union (forerunner of Rugby League) game five days later – a friendly with Tyldesley.

He was a member of Salford's infamous pack of the period, their reputation being never more evident than in the 1899 Challenge Cup semi-final with Hunslet on a quagmire of a pitch at Bradford. Brown and four pack-mates were dismissed, his suspension lasting eight months until January 1900. On returning, he found trouble again when, in Salford's first Challenge Cup final – against Swinton in 1900 – he was reported for kicking an opponent, receiving a *sine die* suspension. Following an appeal, and another eight months of inactivity, he was reinstated in January 1901. Back in the side, he played in Salford's final game at New Barnes in November 1901, followed by the first at The Willows in December against Swinton.

In that match Brown – still seventeen years away from his final appearance – was the only Salford survivor from the Rugby Union days.

Club honours eluded the unlucky Brown. He played in four losing Challenge Cup finals with Salford – 1900, 1902, 1903 and 1906 – and was in the beaten team in the 1904 Championship decider with Bradford. In the 1907 Challenge Cup semi-final – his seventh for Salford – the Reds lost to Oldham and at the commencement of 1907/08 Salford 'announced with regret' that Brown had decided to retire. After a season away it was reported in August 1908 that 'Veteran forward Billy Brown is re-instated by the committee and signed in'. However, after the match at Leigh, on 26 December 1908, he retired again. During the First World War he returned for one match in February 1918, at the age of forty-one, against Broughton Rangers. The match report intriguingly said: 'The old original one and only Billy Brown who, with a "single eye" to his club's successes, was as good as any forward on the field'. He played in three Lancashire county trials but failed to gain selection.

Andy Burgess

Second row forward/loose forward, 1987-1997

Birthplace: Salford
Signed from: Irlam Hornets ARL (Salford)

Debut: 21 April 1987 substitute v. Bradford Northern (away)
Final match: 12 September 1997 substitute v. St Helens (away)

Appearances: 184 (includes 61 as substitute)
Tries: 28
Goals: 5
Points: 122

Representative honours: Great Britain Under-21, Ireland
Club honours: Second Division Championship 1990/91, First Division Championship 1996, Second Division Premiership 1991, Divisional Premiership 1996

When Andy Burgess signed from Irlam Hornets on his seventeenth birthday in April 1987, it was not the first time he had entertained The Willows public. He had already represented his school Ordsall High, as a thirteen-year-old in the final of the Brian Snape Sevens in 1983 as part of Salford's 'Festival of Rugby League' day. After making his first appearance as a substitute against Bradford Northern in April 1987, it was another year before his full debut, at Wigan on 13 April 1988, when he was at loose forward. In 1990/91, he established a regular place in the first team, in what was a special season for Burgess and Salford. He appeared in his first major final in September, when the Reds just lost to Widnes in the Lancashire Cup decider, and the Second Division title – and promotion – was obtained with only one defeat. At the season's end, he was in the Premiership final team at Old Trafford when Salford defeated Halifax.

During the 1993 close-season, he played for the New South Wales club, Casino, but, back in England, he suffered a devastating knee injury in April 1994 that kept him sidelined until the start of 1996. It cost him a place in the team that won the Centenary First Division title in 1995/96, played out as Rugby League realigned itself from a winter to a summer schedule. He bounced back and was a member of the 1996 First Division (formerly Second Division) Championship team – earning SuperLeague status – and appeared as a substitute in the Divisional Premiership final victory over Keighley.

Burgess received international recognition for Great Britain Under-21s, playing in the match with France at Wigan on 15 February 1991 as a forty-seventh minute substitute. In March 1996, Burgess – who has an Irish mother – appeared for the Ireland XIII, invited to meet the United States at Washington's RFK Stadium to celebrate St Patrick's Day. This match led to full international status for Ireland, Burgess taking part in the first against Scotland at Firhill Park in Glasgow on 6 August 1996. He appeared in four matches for Ireland, including two in the 1998 Tri-Nations series with France and Scotland. He played his final game for the Reds at St Helens in a Premiership play-off in September 1997 joining Rochdale Hornets the following year. His testimonial in 1997/98 raised £30,000.

Jimmy Burgess

Second row forward, 1915-1928

Birthplace: Salford
Signed from: Runcorn

Debut: 9 October 1915 (wartime match) *v.* St Helens (away)
Final match: 9 April 1928 v. Barrow (away)

Appearances: 271 (includes 54 in wartime)
Tries: 61 (includes 14 in wartime)
Goals: 95 (includes 5 in wartime)
Points: 373 (includes 52 in wartime)

Representative honours: none
Club honours: none

James Arthur Burgess had to wait an awfully long time for his first official match in a Salford jersey due to the First World War. He appeared in a wartime friendly match at St Helens on 9 October 1915 and established a regular place through the war years, with the exception of 1917/18 when the call of King and Country took precedence. It was not until the home match with Swinton on 15 February 1919 that he finally appeared in a competitive match, three years, four months and fifty-four matches after his debut. He had previously played 11 matches with Runcorn in 1914/15 and was loaned to Salford during the war, being transferred officially in February 1919, when the Cheshire club folded. Over the next nine years, he went on to play in 217 competition games for Salford.

His Reds career, sandwiched between the first Championship in 1914, and the arrival of Lance Todd in 1928, was to cover one of the bleakest periods in the club's history, when the winning of trophies was definitely not on the agenda. It was also a time where there was no recognised kicker at the club and he shared the goal-kicking duties with several players, topping the goal charts, albeit with unusually modest figures, for three consecutive seasons

from 1920/21 with 9, 22 and 24 respectively. Curiously, for a forward at that time, he led the try scoring three times: 1916/17 (wartime fixtures only, with 10), 1919/20 (10) and 1925/26 (9).

With the club not seriously in the hunt for silverware, and no representative honours to his name, his chance of glory was against the touring sides. Unfortunately, he temporarily lost his place in the forwards to George Whitney when the 1921 Kangaroos visited The Willows, but he was in the Salford team that met the New Zealand Tourists on 3 November 1926, the Kiwis winning 18-10. That same year also proved the most memorable for Burgess in domestic terms, Salford eliminating Oldham in a shock away win and then beating Barrow to reach the semi-finals of the Lancashire Cup. After forcing an 8-8 draw at St Helens Recs, Salford had hopes of going all the way, when they replayed at Salford two days later. The Recs had different ideas and won by an unexpectedly comfortable 14-0 margin. It was the closest he came to appearing in a final. After starting the 1928/29 season, he decided to retire and later joined the coaching staff at Salford.

Aubrey Casewell

Second row forward/loose forward, 1928-1935

Birthplace: Welshpool
Signed from: Manchester district ARL

Debut: 25 August 1928 v. Oldham (away)
Final match: 12 January 1935 v. Leeds (home)

Appearances: 187
Tries: 63
Goals: 0
Points: 189

Representative honours: Wales
Club honours: Rugby League Championship 1932/33, Rugby League Challenge Cup 1936 (Leeds), Yorkshire Cup 1935 (Leeds), Lancashire League Championship 1932/33, 1933/34 and 1934/35, Yorkshire League Championship 1934/35(Leeds) and 1936/37 (Leeds)

John Aubrey Casewell was one of Salford's finest back row discoveries from local amateur Rugby League, the teenager first appearing at The Willows for the public trials in August prior to 1928/29. His strong running and tackling caught the eye and the 6 ft 3 in giant – weighing in at over fifteen stone – was signed up and went straight into the first team that month for the opening match of the season, the first under Lance Todd. The fairy tale continued with Casewell having a try-scoring debut in a shock 20-0 win at Oldham. Initially playing loose forward, he later formed a solid second row with Alf Middleton after Jack Feetham took that role.

He made a big impact in his first season and the partnership with Middleton was described as 'one of the most prolific second row combinations the Reds have ever had'. One writer commented: 'Casewell has quite excellent attributes and his harassing tactics serves the side in good stead'. In 1929, he got a taster for the big time as Salford reached the Lancashire Cup final, won 15-2 by Warrington. After two seasons though, he surprised everybody by joining the police force, which necessitated his retirement from the game. After missing the 1930/31 campaign, he returned in August 1931 to everyone's relief at The Willows, but missed the 1931 Lancashire Cup final success in November as he was still struggling to re-establish his first team place. He was in both the 1933 and 1934 Championship finals, however, being victorious in the former, a 15-5 win over Swinton. He became irresistible for defences, developing into a productive try scorer, netting eighteen in 1932/33 and nineteen in 1933/34. The latter is still a club record for a second row forward.

Although described as a local youth when signed by Salford, he was born in Welshpool, North Wales, qualifying him to represent the Welsh in the match with England during November 1932. England won 14-13 at Headingley in Casewell's only international appearance. In January 1935, he transferred to Leeds, winning the Yorkshire Cup with them in 1935 and the Challenge Cup at Wembley in 1936. Uniquely, in the 1934/35 season, his 12 appearances assisted Leeds in winning the Yorkshire League and his 10 for Salford helped them to achieve the Lancashire title. In August 1937, he joined Halifax but after six months moved to Keighley.

Paul Charlton
Full-back, 1969-1975

Birthplace: Whitehaven
Signed from: Workington Town

Debut: 29 October 1969 v. St Helens (home)
Final match: 29 April 1975 v. Wigan (away)

Appearances: 234 (including 1 as substitute)
Tries: 99
Goals: 2
Points: 301

Representative honours: Tourist 1974, Great Britain, Great Britain World Cup Squad 1970 and 1972, England, Cumberland/Cumbria
Club honours: Rugby League Championship 1973/74, Lancashire Cup 1972 and 1977 (Workington Town), BBC2 Floodlit Cup 1974/75

Paul Charlton is probably the finest full-back ever to wear the red jersey of Salford. His strength in defence was equalled by his ability on the attack. He had an eye for an opening that produced a record 33 tries by a full-back in 1972/73. That feat motivated one writer to say: 'Watching Paul Charlton moving into the attack has been one of Rugby Leagues finest sights this season. His speed, fearlessness and hunger for attacking action have brought an incredible number of tries for a full-back.'

His career at Salford was sandwiched between spells as a player with Workington Town, for whom he played 420 times. When Salford tried to tempt them to part with their prized asset in 1969, the Cumbrians drove a hard bargain – and no wonder! An initial offer of £5,000 eventually rose to a Rugby League record of £12,500 before they finally parted, allowing Salford chairman Brian Snape to proclaim: 'I have signed the best full-back in the business'. Charlton, himself, had mixed feelings, but was philosophical: 'I have many regrets at leaving Workington but I think I have made the best move I could to further my career in Rugby League. I am determined to make the Great Britain team to tour

Australia at the end of the season and I feel that by joining Salford my chances could be improved.' That dream looked a reality after his debut against St Helens, as one journalist optimistically wrote: 'Charlton showed why he is the outstanding candidate to tour Australia. He coolly rolled up his sleeves to prevent three tries with strong, perfectly-timed tackling, and linked up enthusiastically in attack with determined running'.

Surprisingly, he was overlooked for that 1970 tour. This was nothing new from the British selectors, and Charlton had only one appearance, against New Zealand in 1965, to his name. At Salford, that situation was to change. He had to be patient though, a substitute appearance in a 1970 World Cup clash with New Zealand eventually being followed by a full recall in February 1972 against France. From then on, his place was secure, and he played 19 times for Great Britain. He appeared in two World Cups (1970 and 1972 – the latter being when Britain became world champions in France) and fulfilled his ambition to tour Australasia in 1974. He played once for England, a 1975 World Cup match against France at Headingley. Charlton had less difficulty in

The attacking flair of Paul Charlton as he outflanks Frank Wilson (a future Salford captain) at St Helens. In support are colleagues David Watkins and Eric Prescott (on right).

making it into the Cumberland team (Cumbria from 1973). Between 1965 and 1979, he played for his county 32 times.

At Salford, he was a member of the 1973/74 Championship team and played in three Lancashire Cup finals, being a winner in 1972, when he scored a try in the 25-11 victory over Swinton. He was also in the side that won the 1974/75 BBC2 Floodlit Cup, but missed the replayed final against Warrington through injury. He appeared in the unsuccessful Players Trophy final bid against Leeds in 1973.

He returned to Workington for a nominal fee as their player/coach in 1975, choosing them ahead of hometown club, Whitehaven, who had also made an offer. 'Nobody is more disappointed than my mum and dad that I am going to Workington. At the moment Workington probably have more potential' he said. From 1976 to 1979, he helped Town to reach four consecutive Lancashire Cup finals, winning the 1977 final against Wigan 16-13.

Paul Charlton is the first to celebrate a Jim Fiddler try in a Challenge Cup tie at Leeds in 1975.

31

John Cheshire

Centre three-quarter, 1955-1963

Birthplace: Wattsville, Cross Keys
Signed from: Cross Keys RU

Debut: 20 August 1955 v. Doncaster (home)
Final match: 9 March 1963 v. Doncaster (away)

Appearances: 255
Tries: 43
Goals: 141
Points: 411

Representative honours: none
Club honours: none

John Cheshire joined the steady stream of Welshmen that had made their way to The Willows over the years, when he joined the Reds from his local Rugby Union club, Cross Keys, in August 1955. He was a strong, reliable centre and, during his time with Salford, built a reputation as a solid defender.

He stayed at the club for eight seasons without gaining any reward at club level. The biggest matches he played in were during the club's Challenge Cup run of 1959, when he was a member of the side that came close to reaching Salford's first post-war semi-final. After drawing 6-6, in a hard-fought quarter-final at Leigh, the mid-week replay at Salford four days later was a sell-out. Unfortunately for Cheshire and Salford, Leigh squeezed through 6-4 after a tensely fought battle. He was in the Salford team that lost 21-5 to the New Zealand tourists in 1955 and played his part in the classic against the Australians during 1959 when Salford went down 22-20. After that match, the famous Australian second row forward, Rex Mossop, acknowledged Cheshire's defensive work after he had twice been on the receiving end of fierce tackling from the Welshman. Representative honours evaded Cheshire and he was unlucky to play at a time when there

was no Wales Rugby League team in action, as he would surely have been in it. He did play for the Welsh XIII, however, against France in Toulouse in March 1959, scoring a try in front of the 25,000 partisan crowd, but it was a match that did not carry full international status.

In December of the 1959/60 season, Cheshire took over the goal-kicking duties. He did not consider himself a kicker but took it on to help the club, following the departure of Syd Lowdon to Workington Town, which left Salford without a specialist kicker. In fact, being a determined and dedicated individual, he worked extremely hard in training sessions on his kicking and even took to practising alone at The Willows on Monday evenings to improve his technique. Consequently, he was the club's top goal and points scorer in 1959/60 and 1960/61, with goal figures of 59 and 53 respectively. During the 1962/63 season, he was moved to the full-back berth, but became unsettled, transferring to Oldham for £700 in March 1963. His career at Oldham never really took off and he played his final game for them in September that year, after only 10 appearances.

Walter Clegg

Full-back/wing three-quarter/centre three-quarter, 1913-1927

Birthplace: Salford
Signed from: Weaste ARL

Debut: 22 November 1913 v. Hunslet (home)
Final match: 8 January 1927 v. Barrow (away)

Appearances: 349 (includes 82 in wartime)
Tries: 28 (includes 14 in wartime)
Goals: 1 (in wartime)
Points: 86 (includes 44 in wartime)

Representative honours: none
Club honours: Rugby League Championship 1913/14

Walter Edwin Clegg made his senior debut at Salford in November 1913. Five months later, he took part in what would prove the highlight of his career. Playing on the wing in only his tenth match, he was in the team that brought the Championship trophy to The Willows for the first time after an epic battle against the great Huddersfield team of the era. Within months, the First World War arrived and things were never quite the same for him at Salford after that.

Signed in January 1913 from local club Weaste – members of the Manchester Rugby League – Clegg played mostly at three-quarter until 1922. Dick Molyneux, signed in 1921 from St Helens as full-back replacement for retired Harry Launce, was struggling and appearing to lack confidence. In a surprise move, Clegg was tried at the back on 16 September at Featherstone. Salford lost 17-3, but he was an immediate success, the match report saying: 'Although playing in an unaccustomed position, Clegg gave a great display. He seemed to have the knack of "bobbing up" just when and where he was most needed and to his determined resistance it is largely due that Featherstone's score was not larger.' Clegg continued at full-back for the remainder of his career.

Alf Beecroft of the *Salford City Reporter*, later wrote: 'Clegg at full-back was an uncanny catcher of the ball. In fact, I do not think I have ever come across his equal, including the peerless Jim Sullivan and Jimmy Ledgard.' Beecroft recalled one particular match, a Lancashire Cup-tie at Oldham in 1926, which the Reds won 3-2 in a mighty upset of form: 'The Watersheddings club had a formidable array of talent and Salford were scarcely more than what would be described as a 'shower'. Salford got a try early on and then had to hold on. Oldham camped themselves in the Salford half for the rest of the game and tried every known tactic to get through, but all their 'up-and-unders' were fielded time after time by the courageous Clegg. He was repeatedly buried under three or four hefty Oldham forwards, but he still had the ball, which he had caught at all angles on a rain-soaked pitch.'

He shared a testimonial with forward Billy Wilkinson during 1928 and in the 1930s joined the Salford coaching staff.

Mike Coulman
Second row forward/prop forward, 1968-1983

Birthplace: Stone, Staffordshire
Signed from: Moseley RU

Debut: 18 October 1968 v. Rochdale Hornets (home)
Final match: 17 April 1983 v. Bramley (away)

Appearances: 463 (includes 22 as substitute)
Tries: 135
Goals: 2
Points: 408

Representative honours: Great Britain, England, England World Cup Squad 1975, Lancashire, Other Nationalities (county), British Lions RU, England RU, Staffordshire RU, North Midlands RU
Club honours: Rugby League Championship 1973/74 and 1975/76, Lancashire Cup 1972, BBC2 Floodlit Cup 1974/75

Michael John Coulman's introduction to the world of Salford Rugby Club was unexpected. As Coulman himself explained: 'I was outside my police house in Staffordshire cleaning my car. I remember it was a beautiful summer's day and I had just a pair of shorts on when this ruddy great Jensen rolled up – it was Brian Snape!'

Coulman had risen through the Rugby Union ranks in spectacular fashion before Snape signed him up for Salford. He started with Rising Brook Secondary Modern School in Stafford and graduated to England schoolboys by 1959 – quite an achievement considering he had not come through the typical education route. At sixteen years old, and still at school, he joined Stafford Rugby Union Club. That same year he was picked for Staffordshire county and, the following year, he was in the North Midlands side. That brought him to the attention of the big Midland-based clubs and he joined Moseley. The next move up the ladder was to play in the England trials, whereupon, after a strong showing, he was in their side to face Australia at Twickenham on 7 February 1967. 'Of all my memories, the most emotional is going out

to play for England for the first time against Australia in front of 75,000 people, and when they played the National Anthem. I was choked' remembered Coulman. He appeared 9 times for England and was on the British Lions tour of South Africa in 1968, taking part in the Third Test match.

He joined Salford from Moseley in October 1968 for a reported fee of £8,500 – a record at the time for a Rugby Union forward. Powerfully built and extremely fast for his size, it was difficult for opponents to hold him once he was into his stride. He fulfilled every Rugby League player's dream by appearing in the Challenge Cup final in his first season. 'I got to Wembley in my first six months and had an awful game. I was slightly concussed but that was not the excuse. If it had happened to me five or six years later, it would have been a totally different attitude for me. I would have taken it in my stride a lot better than I did in 1969.' Although he lost at Wembley, never to return, he could still point to two Championship successes with Salford, but was unlucky when it came to finals, being injured, suspended or ill on several occasions. It caused him to miss the Players Trophy final of 1973, the 1974/75 BBC2

Mike Coulman in full flight for Salford as he evades a would-be tackler.

Floodlit Cup final replay and three out of four Lancashire Cup finals (he won the *Rugby Leaguer* Man of the Match award in his only final in 1976). Happily, he still collected his medals, having played in earlier rounds. He did take his place in the 1976 Premiership Trophy final against St Helens, but Salford lost 15-2.

In 1979, he shared a £17,000 testimonial with Colin Dixon. He blasted his way past Jack Feetham's forty-year-old record of tries by a Salford forward during 1980/81, after having retired at the end of the previous season! However, with Salford's pack being depleted through injuries and retirements he returned to help out, and continued playing for a further two seasons after that. When he finally retired in 1983, that record, still unsurpassed today, stood at 135 tries.

Coulman's first representative appearance in Rugby League was as a substitute for Great Britain in the match against France, at St Helens in March 1971. Subsequently, he played in two Tests later that year against the 1971 New Zealand tourists and appeared five times for England from 1975 to 1977 (including the 1975 World Cup squad Down Under). He also played for the Other Nationalities at county level in 1975 and, after qualification was revised, Lancashire in 1977.

He became assistant coach to Alan McInnes at the end of the 1981/82 season, the pair taking over after Kevin Ashcroft suddenly quit to coach at Warrington, and he retained that post after Mal Aspey took charge in May 1982. Coulman was then handed the role of caretaker coach when Aspey was dismissed in October 1983. 'I did not think I wanted to be coach at first. I slept very little, giving the matter a lot of thought and have decided I'd like to be considered for the position permanently' said Coulman at the time. At the end of the month, club chairman John Wilkinson confirmed his position but after Salford was relegated at the end of the season, Ashcroft returned as coach, a move that effectively broke Coulman's link with the club.

Harry Council

Second row forward/prop forward, 1955-1965

Birthplace: Hyde, Cheshire
Signed from: Dukinfield RU

Debut: 29 January 1955 v. Belle Vue Rangers (home)
Final match: 2 January 1965 v. Rochdale Hornets (home)

Appearances: 262
Tries: 20
Goals: 0
Points: 60

Representative honours: none
Club honours: none

Harry Council, a hard-working forward who loved to take on the opposition with his direct running, gave wonderful service to the club in his ten years at The Willows. His talent may never have reached the rugby field at all for, in his younger days, he was more interested in playing soccer. Tom Bergin, writing in Council's testimonial programme years later, noted: 'He admits that he became cheesed-off with soccer and, on the invitation of a friend, joined the Dukinfield Rugby Union Club as a forward'. That move changed his life and in 1955 he was invited to play in three trial matches for the Salford reserve team, whereupon he impressed the Reds coaching staff and was duly signed up.

At Salford he became the cornerstone of the pack. His versatility was evident in his first season when he played in both the front and second rows with equal distinction, but initially he found his niche in the back row of the pack where he formed a solid partnership with the likes of Hugh Duffy, Bryn Hartley and Roy Stott. In the late 1950s he moved to prop forward where his vast experience led to him becoming the pack leader. As Bergin commented: 'Council became known as the club strongman and it is no more than the simple truth to say

that many times he alone brought victory, by his play and example, or saved the side from a heavier defeat'. Towards the end of his time at The Willows, he was plagued by injuries, including three to the shoulder and the removal of a cartilage. During his final campaign, 1964/65, he was able to play in only two matches mid-season before calling it a day.

Whilst at Salford, he appeared against the 1955 New Zealand team and the 1959 Australians. His outstanding memories include the epic draw at Leigh, in the third round of the 1959 Challenge Cup, and his length-of-the-field try, that brought the crowd to its feet, in the home match against Halifax on 10 November 1956. A great clubman, he was rightly approved a benefit in 1965, the highlight of which was the 'Harry Council Testimonial Match' played on Sunday 4 April at The Willows, when the Harry Council XI met the Television All Stars XI at soccer.

In October 1979, he was one of nine former players honoured by the club at the 'Centenary Match' against Widnes. In front of a near-12,000 Willows crowd, he was introduced to the Rugby Football League chairman and other dignitaries during the pre-match presentation.

Tom Craven
Forward, 1889-1893

Birthplace: Manchester
Signed from: Manchester

Debut: 26 October 1889 v. Broughton Rangers (away)
Final match: 29 April 1893 v. Tyldesley (home)

Appearances: 99
Tries: 5
Goals: 0

Representative honours: Lancashire RU
Club honours: Lancashire RU Club Championship 1892/93

Thomas Craven's finale for Salford was in the concluding match of the 1892/93 season, when a 19-2 victory over Tyldesley clinched the inaugural Lancashire Club Championship for the Reds. It was a fitting note for Craven, one of the club's most popular players, to finish on. He had first played rugby as a three-quarter with the Broughton Park club but then later decided to try his luck at the round-ball version of football for Dalton Hall, Manchester's Owens College and finally with Cheetham Hill. The physical aspect of his first love proved irresistible, however, and he returned to the rugby code with Manchester. He then joined Salford at the beginning of the 1989/90 campaign. Standing at 5 ft 10 in, considered quite tall for that period, he was given a place in the pack, and quickly established himself.

His outstanding form in that first season with Salford brought him to the attention of the Lancashire county selectors at the start of his second term. On 15 November 1890, he made his debut against Northumberland and did so well that he kept his place in an outstanding Lancashire side for the remainder of the 1890/91 season, playing in all eight matches. It culminated in the Red Rose team

winning the English county championship for the first time, breaking Yorkshire's dominance of that period in the process. At the end of the season, he represented Lancashire in the 'Champions' match against the Rest of England at Whalley Range. Having just taken over the club captaincy from Harry Eagles, he suffered a setback in Salford's opening match of the following season. In his first match in charge, he broke his collarbone playing against Barton. The resultant interruption to his campaign cost him his place in the opening matches of the county championship, although he was able to regain his position before the end of that season. He played thirteen times for the county, the last occasion being against Glamorganshire in October 1892.

At the beginning of the 1893/94 season he was named by Salford as a likely starter for their first match of the season, a high-profile clash against Yorkshire club Huddersfield on 2 September. However, he decided it was time to call it a day as far as playing rugby was concerned, having secured honours with both club and county.

George Curran

Hooker/prop forward/second row forward, 1940-1950

Birthplace: Wigan
Signed from: Whelley Central School (Wigan)

Debut: 19 October 1940 v. St Helens (away)
Final match: 30 September 1950 v. Keighley (away)

Appearances: 175
Tries: 12
Goals: 1
Points: 38

Representative honours: Tourist 1946, Great Britain, England, Lancashire
Club honours: Rugby League Championship 1941/42 (Dewsbury), Rugby League Challenge Cup 1943 (Dewsbury), 1951 (Wigan) and 1953 (Huddersfield), Yorkshire Cup 1942 (Dewsbury) and 1952 (Huddersfield).

George Curran was the type of forward worth his weight in gold to any club lucky enough to have him on their books, and he could, and did, play in any pack position from loose-forward to hooker. He was unlucky in starting his professional career in the years leading up to the Second World War, signing for Salford in March 1937 when he was eighteen. His father had been a well-known hooker for Broughton Rangers and the local paper accurately noted, following his trial matches in the reserve side that 'he has inherited all his father's skills as a front row specialist'.

Due to the war, he had to wait until 1945/46 for his first full season. He played predominantly in the second row, transferring to the front row over the next two seasons and finally establishing himself at hooker when Bert Day left in 1948. He was the only Salford player to join his club captain Gus Risman on the 1946 tour to Australasia after playing just 28 times for Salford, although he had guested with other clubs during the war years. On the tour, he played his first match for Great Britain in the Third Test against Australia at Sydney Cricket Ground and was in the one-off Test with New Zealand in Auckland. During the next three years, he was to make four more appearances. He was 'capped' for England 12 times between 1946 and 1949, sharing in two European Championship successes, and represented Lancashire on 7 occasions over the same period, contributing to two county title wins.

He did not achieve club success at Salford but did share honours elsewhere. During the Second World War, he played in four Championship finals as a guest, first with Wigan in 1941 and then Dewsbury in 1942, 1943 and 1944 being a winner in 1942 when Bradford Northern was conquered 13-0 at Headingley. With Dewsbury, he also won the Yorkshire Cup (1942) and the Challenge Cup (1943). He transferred to Wigan in October 1950 for £2,000 and moved on to Huddersfield at the end of 1951. He enjoyed Wembley success with both of those teams – Wigan in 1951 and Huddersfield in 1953, thus winning the Challenge Cup three times, all with different clubs. At Huddersfield, he won the Yorkshire Cup for a second time, in 1952.

George Currie
Forward, 1910-1922

Birthplace: Cadishead
Signed from: Cadishead ARL

Debut: 1 October 1910 v. Hunslet (away)
Final match: 16 September 1922 v. Featherstone Rovers (away)

Appearances: 239 (includes 47 in wartime)
Tries: 2
Goals: 0
Points: 6

Representative honours: none
Club honours: Rugby League Championship 1913/14

George Edward Currie signed for Salford on 27 August 1910, after playing in the pre-season trial games when observed as 'the best scrimmager' on view amongst the forwards. Aged twenty-two and 5 ft 10 in, he was a product of the Cadishead amateur club with whom he had played for two seasons in the Manchester Rugby League. After several reserve games for the Reds, he was given an opportunity in the first team, playing in the pack in the fifth match of the season at Hunslet. Salford won 18-12, ending a three-match losing sequence and Currie made a good impression. One of the reports stated: 'Salford have discovered a man who is better than those who were dropped. He is a player with dash.'

During his first three seasons, however, he could not rely on a regular senior slot, playing in 43 matches and missing the match against the 1911 Kangaroos. In 1913/14, he established a permanent place but did not appear in that season's Championship final victory – having played in the semi-final win over Wigan the previous week – due to sailing to Canada for a pre-arranged holiday.

In the following 1914/15 season, the last official campaign for several years due to the First World War, he had mixed fortunes. Along with many of his colleagues, he was suspended by the Northern Union throughout January after refusing concessions in pay, many of the players feeling they were already poorly rewarded for their efforts due to the difficulties of war. The money was for the 'Relief Fund' to be distributed to players with clubs which were struggling financially. After the dispute was resolved, the Salford lads resumed in February. Currie played his part in Salford's march to the Challenge Cup quarter-final, where they came badly unstuck at Huddersfield, who avenged their Championship defeat with a 33-0 hammering of the Reds.

He continued to play for Salford during the war, appearing in most of the scheduled friendly fixtures until he was required to assist the war effort from 1917. When peace resumed, he recommenced his playing career and from 1919 appeared regularly for the next four seasons, although he missed the match against the 1921 Australians after losing his place for a period to new signing, Teddy Haines. He retired in 1922, almost twelve years after his debut.

Ephraim Curzon

Forward, 1908-1911

Birthplace: Crumpsall, Manchester
Signed from: Manchester district ARL*

Debut: 5 September 1908 v. Runcorn (home)
Final match: 14 April 1911 v. Hull Kingston Rovers (away)

Appearances: 102
Tries: 8
Goals: 0
Points: 24

Representative honours: Tourist 1910, Great Britain, Lancashire
Club honours: none

*Note: the official Rugby League register states Curzon was signed from Kirkcaldy RU, which conflicts with contemporary press reports.

Ephraim Curzon was at Salford for only three seasons but stamped his name firmly into the annals of the club through his selection for the first-ever Northern Union (Rugby League) tour of Australia and New Zealand in 1910. Invited to nominate players considered worthy for consideration, Salford put forward Curzon, Jimmy Lomas, Dai John and Jimmy Cook. A series of tour trials in the spring saw Curzon line up at Wigan on 21 March. He scored a try but, more than that, his scrimmaging and dribbling of the ball – a feature of forward play in that period – impressed and he was in the squad. The selection of Curzon and Lomas for the inaugural tour created much excitement in the Royal Borough – as Salford was then – and on 18 April, the directors held a special dinner in their honour at the Victoria Hotel, Manchester. Fellow players presented 'a handsome pipe each and a stock of tobacco' whilst the directors, ever practical, gave a complete outfit of clothes and cheque each 'to assist them in holding their own with other representatives going out'.

Curzon played in two of the Tests on tour. On 18 June, he was in the first against Australia at Sydney Royal Agricultural ground, Great Britain winning by 27-20 in front of a Rugby League record 42,000 crowd and, a month later, he was in the team to face Australasia – the Aussies including two New Zealanders in their side – at Wentworth Park, Sydney.

Salford fans had their first view of Curzon in the public trials at The Willows before the commencement of 1908/09. After his first match, the local scribe was clearly enthusiastic about the prospects for the new discovery: 'Curzon is a forward of the robust type and a fearless tackler. He is a big local forward of which great things are expected and we should not be surprised if he received county honours in his first season.' His prediction was almost true, as Curzon was in the Lancashire team against Cumberland a year later, the first of three appearances and, in October 1909, he played against the Australians when Salford drew 9-9 with the tourists. Although named by Salford for the 1911/12 campaign, and retained on the register until 1915, he did not appear again for the club, his farewell being at Hull Kingston Rovers in April 1911.

W. (Paddy) Dalton
Second row forward, 1930-1940

Birthplace: Harrington, Cumberland
Signed from: Cumberland district ARL

Debut: 1 November 1930 v. Wigan Highfield (away)
Final match: 18 May 1940 v. Broughton Rangers (away)

Appearances: 291
Tries: 58
Goals: 0
Points: 174

Representative honours: England, Cumberland
Club honours: Rugby League Championship 1932/33, 1936/37 and 1938/39, Rugby League Challenge Cup 1938, Lancashire Cup 1934, 1935 and 1936, Lancashire League Championship 1932/33, 1933/34, 1934/35, 1936/37 and 1938/39

W. Patrick (Paddy) Dalton was discovered playing rugby in his native Cumberland and signed for Salford in September 1930. Following some impressive performances with the reserves, he made his senior debut in the second row at Wigan Highfield in November. It was a wretched day for the youngster to make his bow, the match being abandoned at half-time, but he did well despite the elements. One report said: 'Dalton gave a very encouraging display and should be certain of a regular place'. A month later, he had a second outing in the side to face Keighley and bagged a try in a resounding 44-7 win. It was noted that Dalton was 'another Cumbrian who looks like gaining county honours before very long as he has created a big impression'. Although he became an established member of the Reds' first-team pool, it was 1934/35 before he commanded a stable back-row spot, following the departure of Aubrey Casewell to Leeds.

His natural position was loose forward, but at The Willows that was the domain of Jack Feetham. With Cumberland, however, it was a different story. He first played for his county in October 1933 against Lancashire at Lonsdale Park, Workington. Up to 1938, he represented Cumberland thirteen times – all at loose forward – including the game against the Australian tourists in December 1933. He appeared for England five times, the first one against Australia at Gateshead in January 1934. Later that year, in April, he was in the team for France's first international fixture, played in Paris. When France made a pioneering tour of England in 1934, Dalton played against them for the Rugby League XIII at Warrington in March. Famously, he appeared in the centre for the injury-hit French later in the month against Salford. His biggest blow was in 1936 when he played in the tour trials but failed to make the squad to go Down Under.

With Salford, he was at Wembley in 1938 and 1939, savouring victory in the former and enjoyed the three Championship successes of 1932/33, 1936/37 and 1938/39. In the first of those, he did not appear in the final but contributed to twelve of the league fixtures. After missing the 1931 Lancashire Cup success, he shared in the trio of victories over Wigan in 1934, 1935 and 1936.

Tom Danby

Centre three-quarter/wing three-quarter, 1949-1954

Birthplace: Trimdon, Durham
Signed from: Harlequins RU

Debut: 24 August 1949 v. Liverpool Stanley (home)
Final match: 3 April 1954 v. Workington Town (away)

Appearances: 174
Tries: 61
Goals: 2
Points: 187

Representative honours: Tourist 1950, Great Britain, England, England RU, Durham RU, Hampshire RU
Club honours: none

Tom Danby, an England Rugby Union international, was one of Salford's first big name signings after the Second World War. He was recruited in June 1949 from the Twickenham-based Harlequins club, having played for England in January of that year against Wales, losing 9-3 at Cardiff Arms Park. It was the only appearance by the Durham-born wingman for his country at Rugby Union, after sitting it out on the reserves bench on three earlier occasions.

He made quite an impact in his first season with Salford and, in March, was picked for his first international in the 'new' code, representing England against Wales at Wigan. At the end of the season, he was the only Salford player to be included in the 1950 Great Britain tour to Australia and New Zealand. He certainly did not let anybody down, scoring an incredible 34 tries in only 18 matches. He was included, on the wing, for the vital Second Test against Australia in Brisbane. It was an all-ticket affair, with Australia intent on levelling the series, which they succeeded in doing, going on to win the series. Danby, on his Test debut, had an excellent match. Historian Robert Gate, in his excellent book *The Struggle for the Ashes*

(1986), wrote: 'Within four minutes, Australia were rocked by a gem of a try by Danby. Tommy Bradshaw fielded the ball ten yards inside his own half and broke down the right wing with Danby streaming inside him in support. Thirty-five yards out, the scrum-half passed to Danby, who appeared well covered, but bustled Flannery out of his path, swept past a couple of coverers and accelerated past a despairing Churchill for a try which stunned the crowd.' Danby also played in the third and decisive Test in Sydney and in the second of the two Tests against New Zealand in Auckland.

On his return to England, he represented the tourists in the Lord Derby Memorial match against 'The Rest', played at Wigan in October 1950. He did not play again for Great Britain, but appeared twice more for England at the end of 1950 against Wales in Abertillery and France at Headingley. He topped the Salford try list in 1951/52 with 17 and, in the same season, played for the club against the Kiwi tourists.

In March 1954, he was transfer listed at his own request, at £2,000. An anticipated move to Workington fell through and he took up a teaching post in Sussex in the following September.

Dai Davies
Prop forward, 1936-1952

Birthplace: Garndiefaith, near Pontypool
Signed from: Talywain RU

Debut: 28 October 1936 v. Hull (home)
Final match: 4 October 1952 v. Leigh (away)

Appearances: 370
Tries: 39
Goals: 0
Points: 117

Representative honours: Wales
Club honours: Rugby League Championship 1938/39, Rugby League Challenge Cup 1939, Lancashire League Championship 1938/39

David M. (Dai) Davies had a career of contrasting fortunes with Salford. Prior to the Second World War, he enjoyed the heady heights as a teenager in a Championship-winning combination whereas, post-war, he played out his days as the backbone of a team always likely to finish mid-table. Signed as an eighteen-year-old in August 1936, he was discovered in the Monmouthshire League playing for Talywain Rugby Union club. Barney Hudson said: 'I remember when he joined the Reds from Wales. It can be an alarming experience but Dai quickly settled down. He was especially popular as he was keen to learn and he never ignored a word of advice. Before a practice game, he said that he did not know what a stiff arm tackle was. He had scarcely received the ball when, to use his own words, he "nearly lost his head" in a tackle. As the tackler picked him up, he said: "That was a stiff arm tackle Dai." '

He made his debut at home to Hull in October 1936, playing five matches that season, all in the second row. His second season in 1937/38, was destined to be a bit special. He forced his way into the team in the back row. Harold Thomas, who had arrived from Neath Rugby Union club

during the season, was at prop. For the match with Liverpool Stanley on 22 January, Lance Todd switched them to the benefit of both. At the tender age of twenty, he found himself in the most demanding position of all on the sport's biggest stage at Wembley, in the 1938 Cup Final. Salford won the Cup, and in 1938/39, more success followed as he shared in the double of winning the Rugby League and Lancashire League Championships, experiencing defeat in the Lancashire Cup final and on returning to Wembley.

After the war, he took on the captaincy but there would be no more trophies. In May 1946, he was included in a short tour of France with the British Rugby League XIII, and represented Wales against England at Swansea six months later. His only previous match in a Welsh jersey had been at Bradford in December 1939, also against England. He made nine appearances for the Principality, and in 1952, he received a benefit, making his farewell appearance for Salford in October of that year, after sixteen years at The Willows.

Eifion (Jack) Davies
Stand-off half, 1947-1955

Birthplace: Penclawydd, near Swansea
Signed from: Harlequins RU

Debut: 1 November 1947 v. Keighley (home)
Final match: 20 April 1955 v. Belle Vue Rangers (away)

Appearances: 241
Tries: 49
Goals: 469
Points: 1085

Representative honours: Wales, Middlesex RU
Club honours: none

Eifion Davies, known throughout his Rugby League career as Jack, was a classy stand-off half who developed into a highly productive goalscorer at Salford. He topped the club's goals and points chart for eight consecutive seasons from 1947/48, his highest return being 91 goals and 212 points in 1950/51. He had joined the Reds in October 1947 from the renowned Harlequins Rugby Union Club, having played for several of the capital's best-known teams during the Second World War, including London Welsh and Richmond. When peace resumed, he played in the 1945/46 Victory International series, representing Wales against England at Twickenham – then the home ground of his Harlequins club. Unfortunately, that did not qualify as a full international and Davies did not receive a cap. He also represented the Middlesex county side.

At Salford, he began an enduring half-back combination with Tommy Harrison. It was to be a partnership that would continue throughout Davies' career at the club, although on occasions Davies was moved to the centre, particularly for a period in the late 1940s after stand-off Frank Stirrup was signed

from Leigh. He was not to win any honours with Salford, just missing a top-four play-off place in 1949/50 to Halifax with only scoring difference separating the two clubs. He did appear twice, however, for Salford against touring teams. In October 1948, he was in the side beaten by the Kangaroos and, just over three years later in December 1951, met the New Zealanders. Davies kicked three goals against the Kiwis but the Reds lost to the men in black by 27-12. In both those matches, he played at centre three-quarter.

He gained recognition for Wales in 1949/50 when picked for two of their matches in the European Championship series of that season. The first of those was at Abertillery on 22 October 1949 against the Other Nationalities side. Playing at stand-off, he partnered that wily scrum-half Billy Banks – then with Huddersfield but later to join Salford – and contributed all the points with a try and a goal; but the combined countries just edged it 6-5. His second and final match for Wales was in Swansea against France the following month, although he was reserve for the meeting with England at Wigan in March 1950.

H.C. (Bert) Day
Hooker, 1931-1948

Birthplace: Griffithstown, near Pontypool
Signed from: Newport RU

Debut: 29 August 1931 v. Oldham (home)
Final match: 6 March 1948 v. Widnes (away)

Appearances: 488
Tries: 6
Goals: 0
Points: 18

Representative honours: Wales, Wales RU
Club honours: Rugby League Championship 1932/33, 1936/37 and 1938/39, Rugby League Challenge Cup 1938, Lancashire Cup 1934, 1935 and 1936, Lancashire League Championship 1932/33, 1933/34, 1934/35, 1935/37 and 1938/39

Hubert Charles Day was already a Welsh Rugby Union international – appearing five times in 1930 and 1931 – when Lance Todd first saw him play in the south following a good scouting report. 'It was one of the usual types of Rugby Union games to be seen in that part of the country. But it was not such a bad trip. I signed Day after the game and I think we have been repaid well for our trouble' said Todd.

The former Blaenavon, Pontypool and Newport hooker, turned out to be a reliable performer, his 488 appearances being a club record for official matches until Maurice Richards passed it in 1982. He enjoyed unbroken sequences of 130 games – April 1933 to January 1936, a record before David Watkins' great run in the 1970s – and 101 games (April 1938 to April 1945). In 1938/39, he played 50 times, the most by a Salford player during a campaign. Gus Risman praised Day, whom he signed for Workington Town in April 1948, saying: 'Bert was the quickest striker of a ball I have ever come across, and it was nothing extraordinary for him to get possession from seventy-five per cent of the scrums.'

At Salford, Day shared in many great moments during the 1930s: the Rugby League Challenge Cup finals at Wembley, the three championship wins, three Lancashire Cup successes and five Lancashire championships. He played three times for Wales, each against England, the first being in April 1935 at Liverpool. After the second in 1936, he did not receive his final call until the wartime international at Wigan in March 1945. He was neglected by Great Britain; the nearest he got was a 1932 tour trial match at Headingley. In 1947, he shared a testimonial with Jack Feetham and Sammy Miller, before joining Workington, playing for them five times before retiring.

He later reflected on his career at Salford, saying: 'I think we were at our best by 1937/38. Todd built the team. He bought the best players and knew how to blend them. Most of us played with Salford right through those good years of the thirties and it was only the war that brought it all to an end. I reckon if the war had not come then we could have gone on four or five years with the same players'.

Colin Dixon

Second row forward, 1968-1980

Birthplace: Cardiff
Signed from: Halifax

Debut: 20 December 1968 v. Wakefield Trinity (home)
Final match: 27 April 1980 v. Leeds (home)

Appearances: 418 (includes 9 as substitute)
Tries: 91
Goals: 1
Points: 275

Representative honours: Tourist 1974, Great Britain, Great Britain World Cup Squad 1972, Wales, Wales World Cup Squad 1975, Other Nationalities (county)
Club honours: Rugby League Championship 1964/65 (Halifax), 1973/74 and 1975/76, Lancashire Cup 1972, Yorkshire Cup 1963 (Halifax), BBC2 Floodlit Cup 1974/75, Eastern Division Championship 1963/64 (Halifax)

In December 1968, Salford chairman Brian Snape made the Rugby League world sit up and take notice when he bought two current Great Britain internationals – winger Bill Burgess from Barrow and Halifax's Colin Joseph Dixon. Dixon was signed for a Rugby League record of £11,500, the deal being worth £15,000, as winger Mike Kelly (valued at £3,500) went the opposite way. 'It was a big shock to me when the Halifax directors told me Salford wanted to sign me at a price of £15,000' said Dixon.

Starting as a three-quarter, he had appeared in two Championship finals with Halifax, and was making a name in the back row after developing into a strong-running, ball-playing forward. He had joined Halifax in 1961 from Cardiff International Athletic Club and played for them 245 times. Within six months of signing for Salford, he was at Wembley. In a poor team performance, he was the one Reds player to impress in the 11-6 defeat by Castleford. Having won a Championship at Halifax, he added two more with Salford in 1973/74 and 1975/76, as well as the 1972 Lancashire Cup and 1974/75 Floodlit Cup.

His first representative honour was for a Welsh XIII in 1963 against France, going on to play 14 times for Great Britain (1968 to 1974) and 15 for Wales (1968 to 1981). Apart from touring Australasia in 1974, he was in the victorious 1972 British World Cup team in France, and the 1975 Welsh World Cup squad. He made one county appearance; for Other Nationalities against Yorkshire in 1974. When Les Bettinson resigned as coach in March 1977, Dixon took over. 'To be given the opportunity to prove myself with a great club like Salford, is just like a dream' he said. 'There is no way I will waste this greatest chance of my life'. He found the pressure of playing and coaching too much, however, and resigned after ten months.

In 1979, he shared a bumper £17,000 testimonial with Mike Coulman before retiring after the 1979/80 season. Hull Kingston Rovers then persuaded him to play again and he joined them for £4,000 in September 1980. He appeared 25 times that season, helping them reach Wembley. He was in the final line-up, but was controversially replaced at the last moment. He later coached at Halifax and Keighley.

Hugh Duffy
Loose forward, 1954-1962

Birthplace: Shotts
Signed from: Jed-Forest RU

Debut: 25 December 1954 v. Wigan (away)
Final match: 10 March 1962 v. Blackpool Borough (home)

Appearances: 241
Tries: 51
Goals: 1
Points: 155

Representative honours: Scotland RU
Club honours: none

Scots-born Hugh Duffy was one of the finest loose forwards ever to play for Salford. A quick, skilful ball-player and tough-tackling defender, in any other period he would surely have played for Great Britain. International recognition in an era of great number thirteens such as Vince Karalius, Derek Turner and Johnny Whiteley was always going to be a tough call, although he was reserve in 1959. The only representative Rugby League that came his way was with the Rugby League XIII, on two occasions. The first, on 20 September 1961, was against the New Zealand touring team played, uniquely, at Manchester's White City stadium. A few weeks later, on 12 October, he was in Paris, this time to face a France XIII in the Parc des Princes.

Born in Shotts, Lanarkshire, he made a name for himself in Scottish Rugby Union, with the famous Borders side, Jed-Forest. His reward came on 8 January 1955, when he represented his country in the 'Five Nations' against France in Paris. It was the first international of the season and could have been the start of a long Scotland career but, on the date of their next match against Wales on 5 February, Duffy had swapped the dark blue of Scotland for the red of Salford. He made his official debut for Salford on that day at home to Liverpool City. In fact, he had previously played as a trialist, bearing the unimaginative nom-de-plume of 'McDonald' on Christmas Day 1954 at Wigan, before that single appearance for his country.

Honours were not plentiful at Salford, although he did play in two of the club's biggest matches of that time against visiting touring sides. The first was on 26 November 1955, against the New Zealanders when, unusually, he was in the centre. Playing on a Saturday afternoon, and beaten 21-5, it was the first occasion that Salford appeared in a televised game. The second match, against the magnificent Australian tourists of 1959, was that memorable encounter on 26 September, when Salford went down narrowly by 22-20, with an 11,000 crowd packed inside The Willows.

Duffy transferred to Halifax in 1962 in exchange for Ernie Critchley plus £600, but retained his love for Salford, staying in the city and becoming a familiar figure at the ground after he retired.

Harry Eagles
Forward, 1881-1892

Birthplace: Manchester
Signed from: Crescent (Salford)

Debut: 24 September 1881 v. Dewsbury (home)
Final match: 15 October 1892 v. Broughton (away)

Appearances: 265
Tries: 61
Goals: 0

Representative honours: Tourist (RU) 1888, North of England RU, Lancashire RU
Club honours: none

The most famous player in the early history of Salford was, without doubt, Harry Eagles who, at just 5 ft 6 in tall, was known for his high work rate. Referred to as 'The Genius', he was a born leader, captaining the team in 1888/89 and again in 1890/91. He was always in the thick of the action, urging on the other Salford forwards with his authoritative command of 'Follow me!' One journalist noted he was a 'brilliant, hard-working forward; his dashing example was worth any two men'.

He began his rugby career early, playing in his first match as a fourteen-year-old with Trafford Hornets in 1876. He then moved to the Crescent club, based in Salford, joining the Reds in 1881 when that club amalgamated with Salford. He immediately made an impression, proving to be a consistent and reliable clubman, missing only five matches in the first five seasons he was with them. In 1891/92, his penultimate season and his eleventh for the Reds, he played in all 37 matches. Altogether, he turned out on 265 occasions for Salford, scoring 61 tries in the process. This places him third in both appearance and try scoring lists during the club's Rugby Union era. In the 1886/87 season he was the club's leading try scorer with eight touchdowns.

He was the first Salford player to gain international recognition through his selection in 1888 for England Rugby Union. As England was in dispute with the three other home unions over the new International Board – which England refused to join – he never played. Along with Percy Robertshaw of Bradford, who shared the same fate, he remains to this day one of the only two players to receive an England Rugby Union cap and jersey without playing.

He did receive consolation later that same year, however, when invited to join the first ever tour by a British side to Australia and New Zealand. The tour was a mammoth affair. Departing from Liverpool on 10 March 1888, they were at sea for six weeks before arriving in New Zealand, and did not step foot on home soil again until 11 November. The tourists played 52 matches in total and Eagles appeared in every one of them, a record unequalled in Rugby Union since. It is popularly believed that 53 matches took place on that tour but, in fact, a match scheduled with Northern Districts, in Australia, was cancelled following the tragic death of tour captain Robert Seddon the previous day, drowning in a boating accident in the Hunter

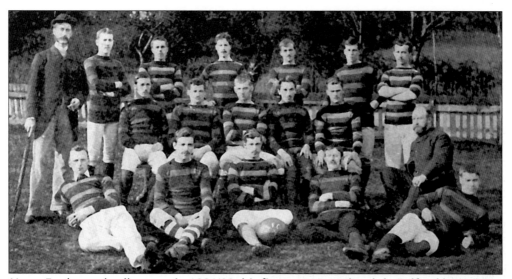

Harry Eagles and colleagues in 1881/82, his first season at the club, Salford having just merged with the Crescent. It is the oldest known photograph of Salford and shows them in their original red, amber and black hoops. From left to right, back row: W.H. Allen (secretary), Sam Williams, Eagles, William Buckley, J. Clayton, Tom Heald, George Hulme. Middle row: R. Bullock, A. Ottiwell, E. Tomlinson, Mick McNally, T. Thornley, John Jackson (vice-president). Front row: F Butterworth, A. Sutton, Hugh Williamson (captain), R.G. McKay, T. Carrington.

River at West Maitland. As the team departed at the end of the tour, one New Zealand writer commented: 'Harry Eagles, who played in every match, was a tower of strength in the forwards.' Another added: 'The muscular Eagles stood out in the forwards.'

His first representative honour came in 1886, when he played for Lancashire in November against Cheshire at Birkenhead Park, qualifying via the Lancashire trial match earlier in the month. From that point on, he became a regular in the county side, making his eighteenth, and final, appearance in the match with Ulster in Belfast during March 1890. He also played in the Jubilee match when Lancashire met Middlesex at the Oval in March 1887, celebrating fifty years since Queen Victoria's accession to the throne. His first major step towards international selection occurred in December 1887, when he was picked to play for the North of England at Whalley Range in the annual, and prestigious, North versus the South clash. These games were looked on as unofficial trials for the England

team and Eagles played in two more; at Blackheath in 1888 and Richmond in 1890.

Club honours eluded Eagles. When Salford won the Lancashire Club Championship in 1891/92, the first team competition that they had ever entered, he was at the end of his illustrious career, playing in just two of the Championship matches at the beginning of that season against Oldham and Broughton, insufficient to qualify him for a medal. He was, however, in the side that met the New Zealand Maori touring team at New Barnes in March 1889.

Outside of his bravery on the rugby field, he received recognition off it with the award of the Salford Hundred Humane Society Medal. This was for rescuing six people from drowning – four from the murky waters of the River Irwell, one in the Isle of Man and another in Belfast Lough. After retiring as a player, he served the club for many years on the committee and spent three seasons as a referee under Northern Union rules.

Alan Edwards

Wing three-quarter, 1935-1946

Birthplace: Kenfig Hill, Glamorgan
Signed from: Aberavon RU

Debut: 21 September 1935 v. Broughton Rangers (away)
Final match: 11 May 1946 v. Oldham (home)

Appearances: 199
Tries: 129
Goals: 29
Points: 445

Representative honours: Tourist 1936, Great Britain, Wales
Club honours: Rugby League Championship 1936/37, 1938/39, 1941/42 (Dewsbury) and 1944/45 (Bradford Northern), Rugby League Challenge Cup 1938, 1942 (Leeds), 1943 (Dewsbury), 1947 (Bradford Northern) and 1949 (Bradford Northern), Lancashire Cup 1936, Yorkshire Cup 1942 (Dewsbury) and 1948 (Bradford Northern), Lancashire League Championship 1936/37 and 1938/39

The 1939 Championship final, decided at Manchester City's Maine Road stadium, attracted a crowd of 69,504 – a Rugby League record at the time. Just as they had several times in big matches during that decade, Salford secured a dramatic, late victory. Castleford were seemingly headed for their first Championship when Alan (some references give 'Allan') Spencer Edwards scored his most memorable try for the Red Devils with just seven minutes remaining. Gus Risman described the moment, saying 'I shall never forget the Rugby League Championship final of 1939. Albert Gear kicked the ball through, and in the twinkling of an eye Edwards was at top speed. He caught the ball without checking his speed and simply flew down the touchline. The full-back, almost in desperation, came across hoping to bundle him into touch. Edwards treated him almost with contempt. As he closed in, Edwards sidestepped in his own imitable style and without checking his breakneck pace went over for a magnificent try. That was Edwards at his very best but then he was hardly at anything else.'

Edwards was another of Lance Todd's Welsh finds out of Rugby Union, discovered, almost by accident, playing for Aberavon. According to Todd: 'I found Edwards while watching a centre at Aberavon'. Edwards had previously been at Maesteg and Bridgend and had had Welsh trials at eighteen. He was nineteen years old when Salford signed him in September 1935. Edwards himself had some misgivings about the move: 'I had promised Todd that if I never grew tall enough for the police I would join Salford. My family were divided, my father wanted me to turn professional but my mother wanted me to wait in case I grew, but I decided to go north. Things were bad in South Wales so you had to do the best you could for yourself'.

To many, he looked too skinny to be a Rugby League player and Risman commented: 'I remember the day when he joined Salford. He had long, thin legs and as we watched him walk on to the field for his first practice, we all shook our heads. This man, we thought, will not last five minutes in Rugby League football. How wrong we were! He turned out to be an incredible winger, and he was the quickest man off the mark I have ever played with or against. He was at top speed in about three strides, and his change of pace was uncanny. So, too, was his change of direction, for Edwards could sidestep, especially off his left foot, without the slightest loss of pace.'

Only two months after joining Salford he was playing for Wales, scoring a try in a 41-7 win over France at Llanelli. Although still not twenty until May 1936, he found himself in the 1936 tour trials. He won his place – to become the youngest ever tourist at the time – and was included in all three of the Tests against Australia, as Britain retained the Ashes, and played in the two wins over New Zealand. He scored 21 tries in 16 matches on the tour but, surprisingly, he played only twice more for Great Britain – in the 1937 series against the touring Australians. He continued as a regular choice for Wales and played eighteen times in the scarlet jersey, the last in 1948, winning three European Championships. He also played for the Welsh XIII against the Northern Rugby League in 1937 and for the English Rugby League versus the French Rugby League in 1946.

His first trophy success with Salford was in the 1936 Lancashire Cup final, followed by the 1937 Championship success. His biggest day with the Reds was in defeating Barrow at Wembley in 1938. He was a loser at the stadium the following year against Halifax and again in the 1938 Lancashire Cup final. During the war years, he guested for several teams, winning the Championship with Dewsbury and Bradford Northern, the Challenge Cup with Leeds and Dewsbury and the Yorkshire Cup with Dewsbury.

After making a transfer request, he went to Bradford for £700 in August 1946. They were at Wembley for three consecutive years, winning in 1947 and 1949 but losing the 1948 final. Edwards missed the 1947 decider, having dislocated a shoulder, but contributed to that success having played in the first three rounds. With Northern, he won the Yorkshire Cup in 1948, losing in the 1948 Championship final against Warrington at Maine Road. In September 1949, he fractured an ankle. He tried a comeback in the reserves but his injuries persisted and his career ended, having made 133 appearances for Bradford.

Alan Edwards photographed at The Willows wearing an alternative Salford kit of a red band on a white jersey.

Flying down the left wing – Alan Edwards chases another try scoring opportunity.

Jack Feetham

Loose forward, 1929-1947

Birthplace: Hull
Signed from: Hull Kingston Rovers

Debut: 21 December 1929 v. York (home)
Final match: 12 April 1947 v. Bramley (away)

Appearances: 409
Tries: 109
Goals: 0
Points: 327

Representative honours: Tourist 1932, Great Britain, Yorkshire
Club honours: Rugby League Championship 1932/33, 1936/37 and 1938/39, Rugby League Challenge Cup 1938, Lancashire Cup 1931, 1934, 1935 and 1936, Lancashire League Championship 1932/33, 1933/34, 1934/35, 1936/37 and 1938/39

Loose forward John (Jack) Feetham was one of the few 'ready made' stars when signed by Lance Todd in 1929, and already an international having played for Great Britain against Australia in the First Test against the 1929 Kangaroos. When Salford tried to prise him from Hull Kingston Rovers, his father advised him to go. 'Dad had worked as a ship repairer in Salford and liked the place' he said. Feetham was watched first by the Rovers when he was fourteen. 'Being a biggish lad for my years, I got a trial as full-back. I got the usual advice to join a junior team and "come back in a year or two". The junior team happened to be a good one. We were known in Hull as the All Blacks of the city. I played as hooker but gravitated to loose forward, and it was in that position that I again went to the Rovers; this time I was a little over eighteen.' He had a try-scoring debut for the Rovers at Wigan in October 1926, appearing 103 times and scoring 30 tries for the Robins over the next three years.

At Salford, Feetham quickly added to his international portfolio and, invited to appear in the 1932 tour trials, found himself in the party to make the trip. On tour, he made four Test appearances, two each against Australia and New Zealand. He said later: 'I think the highest inducement to any young player to train hard and conscientiously, is the possibility of being selected for the Australian tour. It is a wonderful experience and an influence that lasts throughout one's whole life'. It was not all plain sailing however as, against New South Wales at the Sydney Cricket Ground, he was sent off. 'I got my marching orders on the far side of the ground and had to walk right round it to get to the dressing rooms. As I began my long walk the band struck up *Goodnight Sweetheart!*' The following year, he played in all three Tests against the 1933 Australian tourists, although that was to be his swansong as far as Test match rugby was concerned. He made one appearance for England, against Wales at Salford in January 1932, and represented Yorkshire nine times between 1931 and 1935.

For Salford, Feetham played in two Rugby League Challenge Cup finals at Wembley, winning once, four Championship finals, finishing on top in three, and five Lancashire Cup finals, being successful four times. His total of 109 tries created a club

Action at The Willows in 1936 as Jack Feetham (with the ball) is tackled by Logan of Rochdale Hornets.

record for a forward until Mike Coulman passed it in 1980, although his 21 tries in 1931/32 is still the most by a Salford forward in one season. His tackling was deadly, but Feetham had a reputation as a skillful ball player. 'The game would not be half so lacking if loose forwards were sent on the field to play constructive football and not to rampage about on some spoiling mission' he once said. 'Ever since I played in junior football I have had it drummed into me that the real function of the loose forward was to develop movements and not to concentrate only on preventing them. I have scored a lot of tries from the loose forward position.'

In the two seasons immediately after the Second World War, he played in thirteen more matches for Salford although, by now, he was using his guile at prop forward. In September 1947, he came out of retirement to play in a joint testimonial match he shared with Bert Day and Sammy Miller.

In the 1950s he returned to Hull Kingston Rovers as their manager-coach.

Jack Feetham spots a gap in the defence.

Keith Fielding

Wing three-quarter, 1973-1983

Birthplace: Birmingham
Signed from: Moseley RU

Debut: 17 August 1973 v. Leigh (home)
Final match: 17 April 1983 v. Bramley (away)

Appearances: 319 (includes 4 as substitute)
Tries: 253
Goals: 133
Points: 1025

Representative honours: Great Britain, Great Britain World Cup Squad 1977, England, England World Cup Squad 1975, Lancashire, Other Nationalities (county), England RU, North Midlands RU
Club honours: Rugby League Championship 1973/74 and 1975/76, BBC2 Floodlit Cup 1974/75

Keith John Fielding had a meteoric start to his Rugby League career, breaking Bob Brown's forty-year-old try scoring record with 46 touchdowns in his first season. He made his Great Britain debut in January 1974, scoring three tries against France in Grenoble, earning the accolade *'Le Rapide'*. After the match, won 24-5 by Britain, the following report appeared: 'Fielding's tremendous speed brought him another hat-trick and, if form means anything, a trip Down Under. Unless he is struck by lightening – and don't be too sure that it would be fast enough to catch him – Fielding must be the number one certainty for this summer's tour of Australia and New Zealand.'

His overall total for the season, 49, was the best in the Rugby League and earned selection for the 1974 tour, but he withdrew for personal reasons. He had amazing acceleration, giving himself yards before the opposition had time to react. He is probably the fastest ever to play for Salford. Ray Hewson's interesting book *They Could Catch Pigeons* (1996) places his times marginally ahead of the Reds other main contenders: Bill Burgess, Wally McArthur and Martin Offiah.

Fielding's signing from Moseley for £8,500 in May 1973 meant he had to forgo an England tour to Argentina, having represented his country ten times following his debut against Ireland in February 1969 when he was nineteen. Before his first match for Salford he said: 'From what I have seen of Rugby League I don't think it will be difficult to adjust to wing play'. How true that was! After he had helped Salford defeat Wakefield Trinity 22-7 in January 1974, the *Manchester Evening News*' Brian Bearshaw wrote: 'Keith Fielding, Salford's new flier, who scored his fourth hat-trick of the season yesterday, is the most exciting player to come into Rugby League for some time. He has an electrifying effect on the crowd, who automatically get on their toes as soon as the ball starts to get near him. And the ball goes out to his right wing several times in a game, as Salford play to a man who can win a match on his own.'

Although his first official game was at home to Leigh on 17 August 1973, he played seven days previously in a friendly at St Helens, scoring a try in an 18-15 win. His exploits in that initial campaign helped Salford claim their first championship title for thirty-five years, a feat repeated two years later. He appeared in three Lancashire Cup

Keith Fielding flying down the right wing against Wigan in 1979. The other Salford player is Chris McGreal.

finals, although Salford were runners-up in each, suffering the same fate when he appeared with the Reds in the 1976 Premiership final against St Helens.

He could claim glory, however, in the BBC2 Floodlit Cup competition of 1974/75. Having drawn in a scoreless televised final at The Willows in December, Salford had to replay the tie on the ground of their opponents Warrington in January. The pitch resembled a quagmire, and the game took place in driving snow and sleet. But for the fact that the match was being televised, it would almost certainly have been postponed. With the match level at 0-0, Fielding struck decisively, early in the game. One match report said: 'Salford made sure of the trophy in the sixth minute with a try to be savoured. It came with dramatic suddenness. Warrington kicked at goal in the mud, the ball fell wide and David Watkins fielded it, breaking to the right between two defenders. Inside the Warrington half, Fielding was up to take the pass. Outpacing Cunliffe on the outside and holding off all the vainly

pursuing defenders, Fielding raced clear to score.' Warrington never recovered and Salford won 10-5. Fielding, in later years described this as his most memorable try in Rugby League.

He played four times for Great Britain and was in their 1977 World Cup team in Australasia. He also made seven appearances for England – including the 1975 World Cup matches Down Under – and represented Lancashire on three occasions. He also had an outing with Other Nationalities in the 1974/75 county championship.

He became a household name in the late 1970s when he appeared for the first time, and with much success, in the television *Superstars* series. He was Salford's leading try scorer in six seasons and became team captain in 1979/80, leading the side in the 'Centenary Match' against Widnes. Towards the end of his career, he struggled with injuries and then, in April 1983, he was listed at £15,000 at his own request. He almost joined St Helens, but could not agree personal terms and retired.

Albert Gear

Centre three-quarter, 1936-1948

Birthplace: Newport
Signed from: Torquay Athletic RU

Debut: 10 October 1936 v. Barrow (home)
Final match: 24 April 1948 v. Leigh (home)

Appearances: 148
Tries: 40
Goals: 3
Points: 126

Representative honours: Devon RU
Club honours: Rugby League Championship 1936/37 and 1938/39, Rugby League Challenge Cup 1938, Lancashire League Championship 1936/37 and 1938/39

Albert Mark Gear – to give him his full title – will always be remembered for his late try at Wembley in 1938, which brought the Challenge Cup back to Salford for the only time. Tied with Barrow at 4-4, the final was heading for a replay until the seventy-ninth minute, when Gear created history. He later recalled: 'The ball came to our full-back, Harold Osbaldestin, and I positioned myself to keep on-side as he kicked it. It landed in front of their forwards but the bounce was tricky. Troup (of Barrow) was fumbling the ball and he threw out a wild pass. There were three or four Barrow forwards about, and they were hesitating. I was on my toes and running! I kicked it with my left foot and managed to catch it on the bounce. Two defenders tackled me but I was over by about a foot!'

Born in the Newport district and capped for Wales schoolboys, he joined Newport Rugby Union Club but was enticed to Torquay Athletic, which led to an appearance for Devon country. Discovered by Salford scout Ernie Knapman, Lance Todd travelled down to watch him play against Plymouth Albion. He asked Gear to kick the ball so that it bounced into touch. 'I remember kicking the ball towards the corner flag and bouncing it into touch. Whether that impressed him I don't know but I was playing for Salford soon after.'

Aged twenty, he had a try-scoring debut in a 38-0 win over Barrow. He clearly caught the attention of one journalist, who said: 'It was one of the most impressive first appearances I have seen. There was no trace of hesitancy or nervousness. His play throughout gave the impression that he had confidence in his own abilities and he showed that greatest of all necessities for a first-class centre, the ability to go through on his own.'

Gear won two championships medals with the Red Devils, but influenza stopped a Wembley return in 1939. He played his only Lancashire Cup final in 1938, but Wigan won 10-7. His best years were lost to the Second World War. Following his last competitive match for Salford, he made one final appearance on 15 May 1948, against Oldham at Lancaster in a charity match, before ending his career with Belle Vue Rangers.

He played in just ten games for the Rangers, the last – appropriately – was against Salford at The Willows on 1 October 1949.

Ken Gill

Stand-off half, 1970-1978, 1979-1980

Birthplace: St Helens
Signed from: Pilkington Recs ARL (St Helens)

Debut: 11 November 1970 v. New Zealand Touring Team
Final match: 27 April 1980 v. Leeds (home)

Appearances: 275 (includes 4 as substitute)
Tries: 62
Goals: 10
Points: 205

Representative honours: Tourist 1974, Great Britain, Great Britain World Cup Squad 1977, England, England World Cup Squad 1975, Lancashire
Club honours: Rugby League Championship 1973/74, 1975/76 and 1977/78 (Widnes), Lancashire Cup 1972, BBC2 Floodlit Cup 1974/75

In November 1970, an almost unknown, Ken Gill, emerged from the shadows to face the New Zealanders, in England for the World Cup. He had joined Salford two months earlier, and got his chance due to David Watkins being unavailable. Salford lost 8-7, but his performance stole the show. One report said: 'Gill, a neat little stand-off and one of the bright boys in Salford's reserves, made a promising appearance. He emerged creditably, showing good hands, a nice style in running with the ball and a sacrificial daring in the tackle.'

Gill made spasmodic appearances until coach Cliff Evans changed things for the match with Hull on 12 February 1971. As the *Manchester Evening News* proclaimed: 'Watkins has moved from stand-off in a sensational switch. He loses his place to twenty-one-year-old Gill, an unknown amateur player when signed earlier this season'. The adjustment benefited both players and Gill went from strength to strength, most of the team's attacking moves stemming from his repertoire. He won two Championships with Salford (1973/74 and 1975/76) and was in the sides that won the Lancashire Cup in 1972 and the 1974/75

Floodlit Cup. He was in the losing Lancashire Cup finals of 1973 and 1975 but missed the 1974 final through a knee injury. He was also in the team that lost in the 1973 Players Trophy decider.

He toured in 1974, and went Down Under with two World Cup squads (England in 1975 and Great Britain in 1977). He played seven times for Britain, twelve for England and represented Lancashire on seven occasions. He became unsettled at Salford and transferred to Widnes for £15,000 at the start of 1978, sharing in their Championship success of that season. He also played for Widnes in the 1978 Premiership Trophy final, losing to Bradford Northern, having missed Salford's 1976 final appearance through a dispute. His style did not suit the Widnes' pattern of play and, following a disagreement, he was on the move again, this time to Barrow. Sensationally, after only six matches, he returned to Salford for £12,000 in 1979, where his comeback match was a friendly with Leigh on 8 August. His return lifted the Reds' form but, 31 matches later, he decided to retire at the end of the season, citing the prevalence of head-tackling as a factor.

57

Arthur Gregory
Full-back, 1956-1962

Birthplace: Wigan
Signed from: Wigan Old Boys RU

Debut: 18 August 1956 v. Dewsbury (away)
Final match: 30 April 1962 v. Wigan (home)

Appearances: 194
Tries: 28
Goals: 0
Points: 84

Representative honours: none
Club honours: none

Arthur Gregory was signed by Salford in the close season of 1956 with the intention of playing him as a stand-off half, but it was at full-back that he was to make his reputation.

It was in the outside-half role that he made his first appearance in the pre-season Red Rose Cup charity game with Swinton on 11 August 1956, his opening competitive match being one week later at Dewsbury partnering Brian Keavney. After eleven outings the Gregory-Keavney combination was broken up, when Gregory was selected at full-back for the first time for the home fixture with Halifax on 10 November 1956. It had become a problem position for the club and Gregory was the fourth player in five matches tried at the back by the Reds. The idea was a success but the local paper clearly had mixed views, saying: 'The experiment was made of playing Gregory at full-back and that has led to a great deal of debate. It was agreed that he gave a first rate exhibition, with two tremendous crash tackles as the highlights but many followers feel that he has the makings of a future international out-half.'

Despite those comments, and except for the occasional run at number six or on the wing,

he made the full-back jersey his own for the next six seasons. Although he was not to win any honours with Salford, he was in the teams that had memorable cup runs in 1959 and 1961 when the quarter-final was reached each time. In 1959, Salford came close to a semi-final spot before losing a mid-week replay to Leigh at The Willows 6-4. Two years later they went out to Wigan, having led at Central Park with the only try of the first half going into the break. His biggest day was playing his part in Salford's magnificent battle with the 1959 Kangaroos, who won 22-20.

He played in the 1962/63 pre-season public trial match but, when the season opened, John Cheshire was selected at full-back. It signalled the end for Gregory, who drifted away from The Willows.

Gregory was the father of the Lance Todd Trophy winner and future Salford coach, Andy Gregory. In 1958, he was joined at Salford by twin brother Harold, a scrum-half. Although Harold only played in 34 matches for Salford, the pair did appear at half-back together on one occasion – at Bradford Northern on 3 January 1959 when Salford won 15-9. A third brother, Albert, played at full-back for Belle Vue Rangers in the early 1950s.

Alan Grice
Prop forward, 1970-1979

Birthplace: St Helens
Signed from: Blackbrook ARL (St Helens)

Debut: 25 September 1970 substitute v. Featherstone Rovers (home)
Final match: 19 August 1979 v. Workington Town (away)

Appearances: 245 (includes 49 as substitute)
Tries: 4
Goals: 0
Points: 12

Representative honours: none
Club honours: Rugby League Championship 1973/74 and 1975/76, BBC2 Floodlit Cup 1974/75

Alan Grice first appeared in front of The Willows faithful when he replaced Jackie Brennan at loose-forward during half time in the match against Featherstone Rovers on 25 September 1970. Five days later, he made his full debut in another home match against Leigh, playing in the second row. A hard-working, industrious player, the versatile Grice spent the next few seasons in every pack position, including loose-forward and hooker, before finally getting a settled spot at prop midway through the 1976/77 season. An illustration of his adaptability was that in October 1971 he played at loose forward against the touring Kiwis, when Salford won an amazing encounter 31-30. Then, in November the following year, he was at prop against the New Zealand World Cup side, a match that produced an unexpected 50-4 landslide victory.

His first big occasion with Salford was the Players Trophy final in March 1973, when he was in the second row for the 12-7 defeat to Leeds. Later that year he was involved in the Lancashire Cup final against Wigan at Warrington, coming on as sixty-fifth minute substitute for prop Doug Davies, but had to settle for another runners-up medal. He did enjoy the taste of success, however, playing his part in both of Salford's Championship wins of the 1970s. He had a starting place in Salford's 1974 Lancashire Cup final team but again found himself on the losing side, this time against Widnes. He missed the 1975 Lancashire Cup final but was on the bench for the 1976 Premiership Trophy final meeting with St Helens at Swinton. Salford lost, but even more disappointing for Grice was that he sat out the game.

He became unsettled on several occasions and was transfer listed at his own request during 1973/74 at £3,500 and, again, at £5,000 in 1974/75. Each time he had felt that his first-team chances were limited, but he resolved his differences with the club, and was taken off the list. The fans clearly loved him and in 1978/79, he was voted the Clubman of the Year. In October 1979, however, he finally did move on. After finding himself out of favour under coach Alex Murphy's regime, he joined David Watkins at Swinton for £3,000, even though he would have been due a benefit at Salford the following year.

E.C. (Teddy) Haines

Second row forward, 1921-1933

Birthplace: Bath
Signed from: Bargoed RU

Debut: 27 August 1921 v. York (home)
Final match: 7 January 1933 v. St Helens (away)

Appearances: 342
Tries: 56
Goals: 0
Points: 168

Representative honours: England
Club honours: Lancashire Cup 1931, Lancashire League Championship 1932/33

Edward C. Haines – known as 'Teddy' – was a true clubman, spending twelve seasons with Salford, most of them through tough times. He signed during the summer of 1921, throwing in his lot with a team that had come off the back of a season that had yielded only 3 victories from 35 matches – the worst in the history of the Reds. Haines was undeterred and became a firm favourite, playing virtually all his career in the second row. Always willing to exploit gaps in the opposition, he averaged a try every six matches although, during his first season, he registered just one – at Widnes in a 19-3 defeat. In only his second match, he was in at the deep end, facing the Kangaroos who, not surprisingly during that period, won 48-3.

Salford did, however, get off to a promising start in Haines' opening campaign, winning three of the first four Championship matches, more than they had in the league throughout the previous season. Sadly, that momentum was not maintained and his first seven seasons at the club were a battle for survival until the arrival of Lance Todd in 1928.

Haines had already stood out in the Salford pack before Todd came on the scene and was picked to play for England, having been born in the West Country, although signed from Welsh Rugby Union. With Wales as the opposition at The Cliff ground, Broughton, on 6 April 1927, he had the satisfaction of sharing in an 11-8 win in his only international match. The following year, he came close to a place on the tour Down Under. Invited to play in the tour trial match at Rochdale in February 1928, he suffered the biggest disappointment of his career in not making the final squad. He gained some consolation at club level, as the influence of Todd at Salford meant he was now playing for a competitive side. He was in the team that reached the club's first Lancashire Cup final in 1929, although beaten by Warrington, 15-2.

Two years later, in November 1931, Haines – and Salford – were back in the final and this time they were triumphant. Haines played his heart out in the most memorable day of his career. In his final 1932/33 season, he shared in the club's first Lancashire League Championship, playing in eight of the matches.

Tommy Harrison

Stand-off half/scrum half, 1938-1955

Birthplace: Wigan
Signed from: Hindley ARL

Debut: 2 April 1938 v. Halifax (away)
Final match: 8 April 1955 v. Leigh (away)

Appearances: 359
Tries: 62
Goals: 9
Points: 204

Representative honours: none
Club honours: Rugby League Championship 1938/39, Lancashire League Championship 1938/39

There is little doubt that Tommy Harrison would have developed into one of the most famous and successful scrum-halves in Rugby League had it not been for the intervention of the Second World War in 1939. He lost some of the best years of his career, returning to appear in a team whose playing strength had been diluted by the passage of time.

He first appeared at Salford during October 1937, playing as 'A.N. Other' in the reserves at stand-off, signing on the dotted line in November, aged nineteen. The *Salford City Reporter* announced 'The club this week signed the young out-half Harrison, who has been playing well in the 'A' team. He assisted the reserves several weeks ago when he was given a three-week trial and so well did he play, his trial period was extended. Originally a scrum-half, he has struck up a splendid partnership with David Schofield.' His outstanding form in the reserves saw him touted as 'a particularly bright star' but he had to wait patiently for a senior call, eventually appearing in five matches at stand-off during April. After his debut at Halifax, one report said: 'He showed great promise. The ground was unkind to his type of play but his defence was grand and he showed rare pluck.'

He continued to earn a place the following season, playing in just under half the matches, mostly as partner to the great Billy Watkins. He was in Salford's run to the 1938 Lancashire Cup final but not selected for the final itself, won by Wigan. He contributed to the two championship successes of 1938/39; the Rugby League Championship itself – playing in eighteen of the matches but missing the final – and the Lancashire title.

He became a regular first-team choice until the Second World War halted proceedings, returning for the club's first post-war match on 25 August 1945 against Castleford. From that point, he became a central cog in Salford's machine, operating in his original position of scrum-half and taking over the captaincy in the 1950's. In May 1951 he played for a United Kingdom XIII against a French XIII in Paris. However, that was the closest he came to representative honours, although in 1950, his benefit year, he was a 'shadow' reserve for England in the match with Wales during March.

In January 1956, he was removed from the club register, eight months after his final appearance.

Bryn Hartley

Wing three-quarter/second row forward/loose forward, 1950-1961

Birthplace: Salford
Signed from: Salford Juniors ARL

Debut: 19 August 1950 v. Huddersfield (away)
Final match: 2 September 1961 v. Liverpool City (home)

Appearances: 231
Tries: 89
Goals: 0
Points: 267

Representative honours: Lancashire
Club honours: none

Vernon Bryn Hartley had an interesting start to his career at Salford. Signed as a nineteen-year-old on 15 August 1949, he had first appeared in the red jersey earlier that year on 21 May at centre against 'Salford Past' – a match designed to raise funds for ground reconstruction work.

His next first-team outing was a friendly with Blaina – birthplace of David Watkins – on 12 August 1950. Managed by former Salford favourite Jack Gore, the visitors played in the short-lived Welsh Rugby League that sprang up after the Second World War. Hartley's official debut was seven days after that and he appeared seven times in the opening months of the season. All of these matches ended in defeat and he lost his place, being recalled a year later for the home match with Oldham during October 1951. Operating on the left wing – up for grabs due to Syd William switching to full-back that season – he performed well with limited chances, scoring Salford's only try. A report said: 'When a scoring opportunity presented itself he accepted it with alertness and speed'.

From then on, his no-nonsense hard running earned him a regular place as a wing three-quarter. For three consecutive seasons from 1952/53, he was the club's leading try scorer with returns of 24, 14 and 12 respectively. His displays won him selection on the right flank in the Lancashire team which played the Australian tourists at Warrington on 19 November 1952, the only representative appearance of his career.

An unexpected change occurred for the match against Batley at The Willows on 14 September 1957, when he returned to the side at loose forward after being out with an injury. One match report gave his performance a cautious 'thumbs up', saying: 'Hartley, the Reds' former Lancashire county winger, made an auspicious debut at loose-forward but he will come against sterner opposition to test his ability'. Hartley, however, rose to the new challenge and gave valuable service to the club both at loose forward and in the second row, for the remainder of his career. During 1959, he was granted a joint testimonial with half-back John Chadderton. The highlight was a match staged between Gus Risman's team and legendary Australian winger, Brian Bevan's team on 25 May. Gus Risman did Hartley and Chadderton proud, playing the whole eighty minutes despite being forty-eight years old.

George Heath
Forward, 1896-1904

Birthplace: Manchester
Signed from: unknown

Debut: 5 September 1896 v. Widnes (away)
Final match: 3 December 1904 v. Broughton Rangers (away)

Appearances: 227
Tries: 20
Goals: 1
Points: 62

Representative honours: Lancashire
Club honours: none

After Salford resigned from the English Rugby Football Union in 1896, they immediately set about strengthening the side in preparation for renewing acquaintances with the leading clubs in Lancashire and Yorkshire, who had defected a year earlier. In readiness for their first Northern Union campaign in 1896/97, many leading players were recruited by the Reds, none serving the club better than George Heath. He made his debut in Salford's first competitive match under the Northern Union at Widnes on 5 September, quickly justifying his arrival as he became one of the 'work-horses' of the pack.

Salford, led by a fiery set of forwards, of which Heath was a central figure, developed a reputation as a cup-fighting unit, reaching four Challenge Cup finals and a further three semi-finals up to 1910. He missed the club's cup run of 1900, when they reached the final – losing to Swinton – but made amends by appearing in the 1902 and 1903 Challenge Cup finals. Unfortunately, from Heath's point of view, they were both unsuccessful affairs, as the Reds lost to Broughton Rangers at the Athletic Grounds, Rochdale (25-0) and then to Halifax at Headingley (7-0). Whilst Heath and his Salford colleagues continued to be the

'bridesmaids' of the Challenge Cup, it was a similar story in the championship race. In three consecutive seasons from 1901/02, they finished runners-up in the league table – there was no play-off system in place for the leading clubs at that time. On the latter occasion, in 1903/04, they tied with Bradford on points and, although Salford had a superior scoring record, they were instructed to take part in a title decider at Halifax. Once more success eluded the unlucky Heath as the Reds lost narrowly by 5-0.

He did receive some recompense for his efforts from the Lancashire county selectors, the committee picking him for the match against the combined Durham and Northumberland side at South Shields on 5 February 1902. Ten days later he faced Yorkshire at Hull's Boulevard ground, going on to play in five county matches that year and a further four in 1903. After appearing for Salford at Broughton Rangers on 3 December 1904, the Rangers winning 20-5 – the club's sixth defeat in thirteen championship games that season – he suddenly disappeared from the club.

Chris Hesketh

Centre three-quarter, 1967-1979

Birthplace: Wigan
Signed from: Wigan

Debut: 19 August 1967 v. Wigan (away)
Final match: 13 May 1979 v. St Helens (away)

Appearances: 452 (includes 9 as substitute)
Tries: 128
Goals: 0
Points: 384

Representative honours: Tourist 1970 and 1974 (tour captain), Great Britain, Great Britain World Cup Squad 1970 and 1972, Great Britain Under-24, England, Lancashire
Club honours: Rugby League Championship 1973/74 and 1975/76, Lancashire Cup 1972, BBC2 Floodlit Cup 1974/75

When Chris Hesketh discovered he was in the 1970 tour squad, he said: 'For almost as long as I can remember it has been my ambition to play for my country and go on tour. But I thought I had no chance, because when I was seven I caught polio. My legs were spindly and I turned to rugby to build up my strength. It did the trick and that is why rugby will always be more than a game to me.' It was on that tour that Hesketh made his debut for Great Britain, scoring two tries in the Third Test against New Zealand at Auckland.

Later that year he was in the squad for the World Cup, held in England, appearing as a substitute in the final against the victorious Australians, at Headingley. He played in the 1971 series against the touring Kiwis and, in 1972, was in the World Cup squad for a second time for the tournament in France. Hesketh played in the final against Australia, the drawn match being enough to make Britain the World Champions based on the group results. His wonderful defensive effort in that final tie in Lyons had been critical. Another Test series for Hesketh, against the 1973 Australian tourists, was followed by the biggest honour of his career, when he was chosen to lead the 1974 touring side to

Australia and New Zealand. They failed narrowly to regain the Ashes from the Australians but did win the rubber with the New Zealanders. Hesketh's leadership of the team was exemplary and the 16-11 victory in the Second Test against Australia in Sydney with a depleted side was one of the most outstanding performances ever by a British team. He played in 23 matches for Great Britain, 3 for England and 15 for Lancashire.

Hesketh arrived at Salford in the summer of 1967 from Wigan, for £4,000. He had played Rugby Union at West Park Grammar School, graduating to the Orrell club, before joining Wigan. He had offers from Huddersfield, St Helens and Warrington but chose the team he had followed as a schoolboy. Things did not work out and, despite being on the substitutes' bench for the 1966 Challenge Cup final, Wigan coach Eric Ashton – a former schoolboy idol of Hesketh's – told him his chances at Wigan were limited. As a result, Hesketh moved to The Willows. Wigan's loss was most definitely Salford's gain. Jack McNamara accurately predicted: 'The signing of Hesketh, one of Wigan's most promising young centres, should prove a valuable capture, for speed and thrust in the centre has been sadly lacking in what is otherwise a well-balanced team'. Sure enough, at Salford he blossomed as an exciting centre three-quarter, dubbed the 'wriggler' by fans because he was difficult to hold as he dodged his way past opponents. His first outing in a Salford jersey was in a seven-a-side tournament at Halifax in May 1967. A pre-season friendly at Wakefield on 11 August was the setting for his thirteen-a-side debut, followed by his first competitive match at Wigan in the Lancashire Cup the following weekend.

In his second season at Salford, he was back at Wembley but this time he was in the starting line-up. He came away a loser, being the only Reds player to touch the ball down over the Castleford line. Sadly, for Hesketh and Salford, it was ruled a 'double movement' by the referee. In 1972, he shared in the triumph of winning the club's first silverware since 1939, when the Lancashire Cup was secured after defeating old rivals Swinton at Warrington. The championship followed, in dramatic fashion during a make-or-break Easter programme, in 1973/74. Salford repeated that success in 1975/76, but on the second occasion Hesketh could take pride in being the team captain, having taken over from David Watkins in 1974. He also led the side, when they lifted the Floodlit Trophy in January 1975. He was a runner-up in the finals of the Lancashire Cup in 1973 and 1975, the Players Trophy in 1973 and the Premiership Trophy in 1976. He missed the 1974 Lancashire Cup final through a knee injury.

Former club statistician and programme editor Bert Hughes captured the enthusiasm and professionalism of Hesketh when, in 1983, he wrote: 'In April 1971 Salford needed league points at Swinton to ensure a home tie in the first round of the championship play-off, while Swinton were chasing a qualifying spot. The scene was set at Station Road for a particularly keen contest between the derby rivals. As the final minutes ticked away, and with the score at 20-18 in the Lions' favour, Salford were awarded a penalty and opted for a goal attempt to draw the game and salvage a point. Reds winger Paul Jackson teed up the ball and booted it but, to the Reds' dismay, it

Muddied captain Chris Hesketh lifts the 1974/75 BBC2 Floodlit Trophy in triumph after victory over Warrington in the final.

hit a post and rebounded into play. Then, like something out of *Boy's Own*, a red-clad figure flashed through the Swinton ranks, gathered the ball and touched down between the posts. Chris Hesketh had been rewarded for the innumerable times he had followed up penalty kicks, and the day's honours went to Salford.'

Hesketh took over as caretaker coach after Colin Dixon quit the role in January 1977, holding the reins until Stan McCormick arrived on the scene a few weeks later. He received an MBE in the 1976 New Year list and, in 1978, shared a £12,600 testimonial with Watkins. After finishing at Salford, he moved to Swinton on a free transfer in September 1980, but retired without playing a game. 'I have been troubled with a neck injury for some time and decided it wasn't worth the risk. I have no arguments with Swinton' he said.

Barney Hudson

Wing three-quarter, 1928-1946

Birthplace: Horden, Durham
Signed from: Hartlepool Rovers RU

Debut: 6 April 1928 v. Wigan Highfield (home)
Final match: 22 April 1946 v. Wigan (home)

Appearances: 411
Tries: 282
Goals: 58
Points: 962

Representative honours: Tourist 1932 and 1936, Great Britain, England
Club honours: Rugby League Championship 1932/33, 1936/37, 1938/39 and 1941/42 (Dewsbury), Rugby League Challenge Cup 1938 and 1943 (Dewsbury), Lancashire Cup 1931, 1934, 1935 and 1936, Yorkshire Cup 1942 (Dewsbury), Lancashire League Championship 1932/33, 1933/34, 1934/35, 1936/37 and 1938/39

Bernard Hudson – known by all as Barney – is a true legend of the Salford club. A colourful personality, he is remembered with great affection at The Willows. When Salford needed inspiration, the cry was always 'Give it to Barney!' He took the bold step, at twenty-two, of leaving his County Durham home for Salford in April 1928. 'I got a nominal signing-on fee. The main thing, however, was a job. I wanted to get out of the pit and Salford fixed me up with an engineering job' he said. Signed on Good Friday, he made his debut the same day against Wigan Highfield, playing three matches during his first four days at the club! In the third, at Barrow on Easter Monday, he scored his first and second tries towards a Salford career total of 282 – a club record until overtaken by Maurice Richards in 1983.

Gus Risman described what a threat Hudson was to the opposition. 'Contrary to the general rule, the older Barney got, the better player he became. As the years went on, he developed more speed and more precision of movement. In the early days of his career he could see just one thing – the line. He would go straight for the line – and I do mean straight. The fact that a couple of opponents were positioned between him and the line meant absolutely nothing. He developed not only a sidestep, but a devastating hand-off. When in full flight, his impact was akin to a hydrogen bomb.' Hudson was selected as a tourist in both 1932 and 1936, and, in the latter, took part in the historic final Test victory over Australia at Sydney Cricket Ground when four of his Salford team-mates shared the glory. In total, he made eight appearances for Great Britain and earned further recognition by playing six times for England.

With Salford, he played at Wembley in 1938 and 1939, won winner's medals from three Rugby League Championships, five Lancashire League Championships and four Lancashire Cup victories (he missed the 1936 final through a leg injury but still got his medal). During the Second World War, he had success as a guest player with Dewsbury, who he captained, winning the championship in 1941/42, the Yorkshire Cup in 1942 and the Challenge Cup in 1943. After retirement in 1946, he later joined the coaching staff at Salford.

James Jackson
Forward, 1882-1886

Birthplace: Chepstow
Signed from: Leigh

Debut: 14 October 1882 v. Eccles (home)
Final match: 20 March 1886 v. Manchester Free Wanderers (home)

Appearances: 59
Tries: 8
Goals: 0

Representative honours: Lancashire RU
Club honours: none

James Jackson played only 59 matches for Salford, but he had a significant part in the early history of the club. His selection for Lancashire in 1886 was a breakthrough that opened the gates for others to follow. At that time, there was no competitive club rugby and therefore no team honours. The measure of a club's standing was the number of players seen in international or county caps and jerseys on team photographs. Despite Salford being virtually unbeatable as a team, the county committee continually overlooked the claims of the players on the basis that they possessed 'no individual merit'. After Jackson infiltrated the county ranks, that theory evaporated.

Everything changed when the twenty-seven-year-old played against Durham on 30 January 1886. He had been selected for the match with Yorkshire at Huddersfield the previous November, but withdrew due to illness. Although he could have probably played, he did not want to risk a below par performance and jeopardise the chances of his colleagues being selected in future. His decision was vindicated, with a fine display against Durham clearing the path for eight more Salford players to make county debuts over the next three seasons. The prestige that

it gave the club also resulted in an improved fixture list and a seat on the county committee.

Jackson began playing rugby in his hometown of Chepstow, on the Monmouthshire coast, as a half-back when he was sixteen. After two years at Caermarthan College, he obtained a job as a schoolmaster in Leigh during 1879. He joined the Leigh club, becoming team captain, a position he fulfilled for two years before transferring to Salford in 1882. After just one reserve game for Salford, he was promoted to the first team. Starting in the three-quarter line, he moved into the pack due to an absentee and remained there. Standing at 5 ft 10 in and weighing twelve stone, Jackson was considered to have a good physique for that time. Due to his outstanding club performances, he had been nominated often for Lancashire, but the claim was continually overlooked, although he was a reserve for the Lancashire-Yorkshire match at Whalley Range in November 1884. His final match for Salford was against the Manchester Free Wanderers on 20 March 1886, Jackson failing to appear for a later fixture against Manchester in April.

Emlyn Jenkins

Stand-off half, 1930-1938, 1940

Birthplace: Treorchy
Signed from: Cardiff RU

Debut: 6 December 1930 v. Dewsbury (home)
Final match: 7 December 1940 (as guest) v. Leigh (home)

Appearances: 246
Tries: 88
Goals: 44
Points: 352

Representative honours: Tourist 1936, Great Britain, Wales, England, Other Nationalities
Club honours: Rugby League Championship 1932/33 and 1936/37, Lancashire Cup 1931, 1934, 1935 and 1936, Lancashire League Championship 1932/33, 1933/34, 1934/35 and 1936/37

On Easter Saturday 1937, Salford met their derby rivals Swinton in a vital championship match at The Willows in front of a 16,000 crowd. It was a crucial game for Salford, with a top four play-off place at stake and the Lancashire League Championship up for grabs. On a waterlogged ground, ankle-deep in mud as a result of a heavy snowfall the previous day, the teams played out the match in a cup-tie atmosphere, Salford eventually finishing on top 13-0. In the post-match analysis, one journalist wrote: 'One player stood out above all others – Emlyn Jenkins. He was at his very best, and when I say that, you realise how good he was. His kicking was beautifully timed and not overdone. Repeatedly he set his three-quarters in motion. Invariably he made ground before parting with the ball and constantly he schemed to launch attack after attack.' This summed up the match-winning qualities of Jenkins, one of the quickest, most gifted and unorthodox half-backs to emerge from the valleys of Wales.

A Welsh schoolboy Rugby Union international, he began his career in 1928 with Treherbert, moving on to Bridgend in 1929 and finally joining Cardiff during 1930. He came close to his dream of representing his country in April 1930, when he was a non-playing reserve for Wales in Paris. At the end of the year, he was in line for a place once more, but Jenkins claimed in later years that Lance Todd deprived him of a possible cap. Jenkins was on stand-by to replace Windsor Lewis of Maesteg in the final trial in December 1930. Lewis withdrew with an injury and Jenkins was called to replace him but, according to Jenkins, Todd kept the news from him by getting him on the train north to sign with Salford before he found out. 'You can call it cleverness on Todd's part, but it always stuck in my throat' said Jenkins. Nonetheless, Jenkins respected Todd as a manager but, then again, it was probably a wise idea. As Jenkins himself said: 'Todd would bring a point home in dramatic fashion and he once did it to me at Warrington. I had been getting clobbered so I began to kick, which was stupid of me because there was a high wind. Even Gus Risman had a word with me about it. At half time, in walked Todd with a shovel full of red-hot coals from the boiler. Todd asked "Where is that little so-and-so? Take off your boot and I will fill it! That'll stop you so-and-so kicking!"'

Jenkins had his introduction to Great Britain in the Third Test against Australia at Swinton in December 1933, sharing a debut with Salford half-back partner Billy Watkins. He was selected for the 1936 tour to Australia and New Zealand with four of his Salford comrades, including Watkins. Writing about the pair, Risman commented: 'Jenkins and Watkins were the half-backs to end all half-back combinations. Never have I known a pair of footballers with such a complete understanding, and it was around this pair that most of our moves revolved in the Salford heyday. They practised together until they knew each other inside out. The mere lifting of an eyebrow, the slightest movement of a finger, all meant something in the Jenkins-Watkins code.'

Following the 1936 series in Australia, won by Great Britain, one Australian scribe said: 'Jenkins was the outstanding player in all three Tests and tricked the Australian inside men repeatedly with skilful and varying tactical moves. He undoubtedly surpassed himself and rose to magnificent heights.'

Although Jenkins missed his Welsh Rugby Union cap, he had a varied international career in Rugby League. All told, he played in nine Test matches for Britain and turned out for Wales four times, including being a member of the side that won the 1936/37 European Championship. He again represented the Principality when he played for a Wales XIII against the Northern Rugby League at Newcastle in April 1937. Another international calling was for the Other Nationalities side that met England at Lonsdale Park, Workington, in March 1933. Bizarrely, having already played against them on two occasions, he was then asked to play for England twice during 1934. The first was against the Australian touring side at Gateshead in January, and the second when he travelled to Paris in April for the first-ever international match played by France.

Jenkins suffered a loss of form during the 1937/38 season and was dropped from the team, resulting in a 'war of words' with Todd, as he felt he was being made a scapegoat for some poor results by the team. A transfer request was, initially, rejected by the board. It was finally resolved when Jenkins joined Wigan in March 1938 for £1,000, his final game for Salford being on 29 January 1938 at Broughton Rangers, when

Emlyn Jenkins, wearing Salford's alternate strip of a white jersey with a red band, poses for the camera at the conclusion of a seven-a-side tournament.

he scored the only try in a 3-7 reversal. It meant that he missed a potential trip to Wembley with Salford later that year, although he could still reflect on a glorious career with Salford, winning the Rugby League Championship in 1932/33 – when he scored a try in the 15-5 final win over Swinton – and in 1936/37. He also played his part in the four Lancashire Cup victories of that period. Apart from Wigan, he also had brief spells with Keighley, Bradford Northern and Leigh, coaching the latter after the Second World War. He did return to Salford as a guest player, for one final match against Leigh at The Willows in December 1940. Lining up with his old pal Watkins for one last time, he scored a try in the 38-0 win. It was almost ten years to the day after his debut.

Dai John

Stand-off half/scrum half, 1905-1922

Birthplace: Penygraig, near Tonypandy
Signed from: Penygraig RU

Debut: 21 January 1905 v. Leeds (away)
Final match: 25 February 1922 v. Barrow (away)

Appearances: 455 (includes 49 in wartime)
Tries: 49 (includes 8 in wartime)
Goals: 95 (includes 49 in wartime)
Points: 337 (includes 122 in wartime)

Representative honours: Wales
Club honours: Rugby League Championship 1913/14

William David (Dai) John was described as 'the Prince of half-backs and an established favourite with the crowd on every field in which he makes his appearance.' John was one of the most exciting players Salford had on their books in the years before the First World War. He was a 5 ft 2 in pocket dynamo, who weighed in at ten and a half stone and ran like a whippet. He arrived unheralded from South Wales in 1905, and created a half-back pairing with Dave Preston that would mesmerise defences for the next three years, until John was controversially moved to full-back in November 1908. It was a position the club tried to fill for several years and, in desperation, they had turned to the reliable Welsh wizard.

One writer, summing up his impact at the back said: 'By his dash and smartness, his speed and resource, the little Welshman built up for himself a reputation seldom equalled. He really proved himself in spite of, and in fact with, the assistance of methods not always considered orthodox, especially by the other sides'. It was noted at the time that: 'He is so capable a full-back that a large sum was offered for his transfer and his name was included amongst the leading candidates for the tour of Australia'. John did play at full-back in the tour trial match at Wigan in March 1910 but was not included in the final squad.

Halfway through the 1910/11 season, he resumed at half-back, playing scrum-half, with Edgar May now established as his regular partner. It was a combination that took Salford to their first championship success in 1914, the 5-3 win in the decider with Huddersfield making up for the disappointment of 1906 when he was in the side beaten by Bradford in the Challenge Cup final.

In spite of his glowing reputation and versatility, he had precious few representative chances. His first opportunity was in September 1906, playing in the Lancashire county trial at Broughton Rangers' ground. He earned a place as reserve for the match with Cumberland in Maryport the following month, but that was as close as he came to county selection. In February 1913, he finally received his due, when he was chosen to play full-back for Wales against England in Plymouth.

Graham Jones

Stand-off half/wing three-quarter, 1954-1962

Birthplace: Penarth
Signed from: Penarth RU

Debut: 27 November 1954 v. Leigh (home)
Final match: 4 May 1962 v. Leigh (home)

Appearances: 239
Tries: 119
Goals: 0
Points: 357

Representative honours: none
Club honours: none

Graham Jones equalled a post-war club record in 1959/60 when, operating on the right wing, he matched George Aspinall's 1947/48 return of 27 touchdowns for a season. It was a total not overtaken until fellow Welshman Maurice Richards scored 35 in 1971/72. For Jones, it was an unlikely outcome, having been signed by Salford as a stand-off half from the Penarth Rugby Union club in 1954 as a potential replacement for the previous incumbent, Jack Davies. After three years, however, it was felt that his exceptional pace and side-step was better suited to that of a wing three-quarter and he played there permanently from November 1957.

Jones suffered – along with other talented Welsh Rugby League players – through the fact that a Wales international side did not take to the field between 1953 and 1968. There were, however, a few instances where a Welsh XIII was selected, one of those being on 1 March 1959 for a match against France in Toulouse. He was picked to play at stand-off with Wigan's Rees Thomas at scrum-half. He had plenty of company, with Salford colleagues John Cheshire and George Parsons included as well as a former Red, Dai Moses.

Jones scored a try but Wales lost 25-8. The match did not have full international status and, consequently, no caps were awarded. With a bumper crowd of 25,000 at the game, it is difficult to understand why the Wales team was not resurrected until nine years later.

Jones registered the first of his 119 tries on 27 December 1954 at home to Whitehaven in a 6-6 draw, playing at stand-off. In his second season at The Willows, he was in the Salford side that met the New Zealand tourists in November 1955 and four years later, in September 1959, he was involved in a nail-biter against the Australian tourists. Jones had put the Reds 10-7 ahead just before half-time, taking a superb pass on the wing from his centre partner Bob Preece, but the visitors finally won 22-20. Although he had a fine season in 1961/62, where he was Salford's top try scorer for the second time with 18, scoring two 'hat-tricks' into the bargain, he played his last match at the end of that season. Including the pre-season 'Red Rose Cup' game with Swinton, he had turned out 39 times during the campaign.

James Jones
Forward, 1894-1896

Birthplace: Manchester
Signed from: Manchester Rangers

Debut: 27 January 1894 v. Rochdale Hornets (home)
Final match: 14 November 1896 v. Tyldesley (away)

Appearances: 54
Tries: 6
Goals: 0
Points: 18

Representative honours: Lancashire RU
Club honours: none

The old maxim 'He came, he saw, he conquered' could be a very apt description for forward James J. Jones who, during his thirty-four months with Salford, appeared 12 times for Lancashire. He arrived in January 1894 from Manchester Rangers and it was noted that, as a player 'he had a first-class reputation having established it at Durham University'. At Salford he made a sensational start and, after only three matches for the club, he represented Lancashire against the Midland Counties at Moseley on 21 February, followed by an appearance against Somerset at Whalley Range in March.

Salford was looking to Jones, and several other mid-season acquisitions, to turn things round as they had struggled to maintain the momentum of winning the inaugural Lancashire Club Championship the previous term. His signing did not halt the slide but he certainly made an impression. Salford relinquished their prize, but 1894/95 started on a more optimistic note, Jones scoring his first points for Salford with a try in the 33-0 seven-try demolition of Sale in the opening match. The following week they registered nine tries against his former club, Manchester Rangers, who were overrun 34-3. Then, with

the season barely six weeks old, things went badly wrong for Salford and Jones. The club was suspended on 16 October for alleged professionalism, the charge being that they induced Joe Smith, a Radcliffe three-quarter, to play for them by giving him weekly payments. The ban lasted until January 1895 and for the players, Jones in particular, it meant they could not represent the county. This cost him, potentially, four county caps.

On New Year's Day 1895, Salford returned to action but were out of the Lancashire Championship, having been scrubbed from the competition as a result of their misdemeanours. Happily for Jones, he quickly regained his Lancashire place and was a member of the side to make the West Country tour in March playing Devon at Exeter and Glamorgan at Cardiff. The following season, 1895/96, he appeared in a further eight matches for the county. At the end of that campaign, Salford resigned from the RFU. Jones, having made 44 appearances under Rugby Union rules for Salford, continued for a further ten under the Northern Union banner before disappearing from the picture in November 1896.

Brian Keavney

Scrum-half, 1951-1958

Birthplace: Leigh
Signed from: Leigh St Joseph's ARL

Debut: 4 April 1951 v. Rochdale Hornets (home)
Final match: 16 August 1958 v. Bradford Northern (home)

Appearances: 169
Tries: 31
Goals: 104
Points: 301

Representative honours: Lancashire
Club honours: none

Brian Keavney was one of the most exciting scrum-half backs seen in the red jersey and another unsung hero who could have gained greater recognition had he been with a club more fashionable than Salford was in his playing days. A typical stocky, clever and determined half-back, he gained his only county cap against the 1955 New Zealand tourists on 12 October. He played at Warrington, where Lancashire lost narrowly 17-15, Keavney's partner at stand-off being Swinton's Albert Blan, later to make a name for himself as a back row forward. A month later, on 26 November, Keavney took on the Kiwis again, but this time wearing Salford colours. Despite scoring a goal, he found himself on the wrong end of a 21-5 score line.

The following season, 1956/57, was probably his best, personally, with Salford. He finished up as the club's top try scorer on 15, the leading goalscorer with 63 and, consequently, the top points scorer, registering 171. He also received his one other representative call, when chosen for the Rest of the League to play Great Britain in October at Bradford, as part of Britain's preparation for the arrival of the Australian tourists.

A product of Leigh junior Rugby League, he made an end-of-season debut against Rochdale in April 1951, covering for the unavailable Tommy Harrison, with Jack Davies at stand-off. He had to wait until the following season to play again, making just 5 starts in 1951/52 and then 14 in 1952/53, scoring his first try on 24 January that season in a 37-4 win at Liverpool City. He continued to share the number seven jersey with Harrison, but finally took over when Harrison finished midway through the 1954/55 season. With Davies also retiring, and there being no specialist goal-kicker, Keavney inherited some of the kicking duties in 1955. Incredibly, he finished as the top marksman in 1955/56 with just 25 – being one of seven Salford players to kick goals that season!

The arrival of scrum-half Harold Gregory – brother of full-back Arthur – at the start of 1958/59 saw Keavney moved to stand-off, but he decided not to stick around. After the opening two matches, one a pre-season friendly, he transferred to Widnes in September. At Widnes, he partnered Frank Myler for over three seasons, playing in 96 matches for the Chemics.

Tom Kent

Forward, 1887-1894

Birthplace: Nottingham
Signed from: Radcliffe

Debut: 17 September 1887 v. Rochdale Hornets (home)
Final match: 28 April 1894 v. Barton (home)

Appearances: 169
Tries: 18
Goals: 2

Representative honours: Tourist (RU) 1888, England RU, North of England RU, Lancashire RU
Club honours: Lancashire RU Club Championship 1892/93

Thomas Kent has the unique distinction of being the only player from the Salford club to represent England at Rugby Union. In the days before France arrived on the scene to create the annual Five Nations Championship series, Kent appeared in all six of England's home internationals during 1891 and 1892. His historic first match – from a Salford point of view – was against Wales at Newport on 3 January 1891. England won that particular encounter 7-3 and he was in the side which then defeated Ireland 9-0 in Dublin the following month, failing at the final hurdle to collect the title through losing to Scotland at Richmond. The following year, however, he was to share in England's Triple Crown success, playing in victories over all three countries: Wales 17-0 (at Blackheath), Ireland 7-0 (Whalley Range) and Scotland 5-0 (Edinburgh). Kent had frustratingly been the first reserve forward, sitting it out for the internationals against Scotland and Ireland in 1890, before he finally got his chance.

The *Athletic News*, commenting on Kent's contribution to the England effort, wrote: 'He played with the same old dash. A fine, energetic, forward, very quick at following up, and tackles surely. He never seemed to tire.' Salford secretary James Higson said about Kent: 'He has always been a hard-working forward, his weight and activity telling in his favour, and his quick following up has earned the club many a try. In consequence of his energy, he receives many a knock, but he soon recovers, and comes up again like a Briton – or a Salfordian!'

Kent had already contributed to the pioneering 1888 tour of Australia and New Zealand. He was quick off the mark, scoring the opening try of the tour in the first game against Otago, played at the Caledonian Ground in Dunedin. According to a match report, he scored by the posts after 'a splendid bout of passing from a throw-in'. Kent's first recognition had come earlier in 1888, with his selection for Lancashire against Durham at the Hartlepool ground in January. His consistent and impressive form during the next few years was evident from the fact that he was to make a total of 33 appearances for Lancashire – a record number for a Salford player under any code of rugby – and he was virtually an ever-present member of the side until 1893. The most memorable season for Kent in the county colours was when he played his part in Lancashire's county championship success of 1890/91, something they could not repeat until

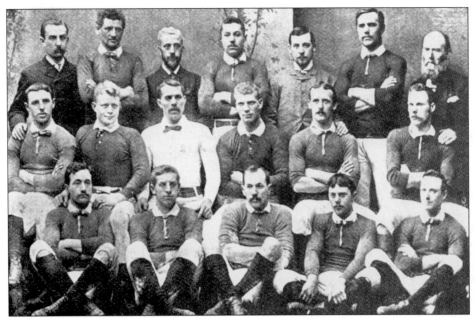

Tom Kent with the magnificent Salford team of 1887/88 that lost just 6 matches out of 35. From left to right, back row: L.J. Reynolds (treasurer), A. Ottiwell, D. Wellwood (chairman), Jack Roberts, James Higson (secretary), J. McVittie, J. Horrocks (vice-president). Middle row: Joe Shaw, Jack Anderton, Harry Eagles, Kent, George Jackson, A.E. Ogden. Front row: J. Newton, H.H. Clegg, Sam Williams, William Manwaring, Herbert Cook.

1935 – due in no small way to the breakaway of the northern clubs from the Rugby Football Union in 1895. At the end of their championship season, Lancashire took on the Rest of England at Whalley Range, in what was then a traditional climax to the season. Kent, along with his Salford colleague Tom Craven, played in the match, which ended in a victory for the Rest team. Soon after his Lancashire debut, he gained selection for the North of England in the clash against the South of England. These matches, played annually, had a high profile at the time, being just one tier below international recognition. The first of what would be three appearances for Kent was in February 1888 at Blackheath.

Kent had joined Salford from Radcliffe and made his first appearance in the opening match of the 1887/88 campaign. Playing at half-back against Rochdale Hornets, he scored the match-winning drop-goal. It was, rather curiously, to be the only one he scored in his

169 matches for the Reds. The following week he played in the forwards, where he was to stay for most of his career with Salford, except for the odd game in the three-quarters or at half-back. At Salford, he made an instant impression with his forward play, resulting in his selection for the 1888 tour at the season's end.

During 1888/89 – shortly after returning from the arduous tour of Australia and New Zealand – he decided to return to Radcliffe, playing just five times for Salford that season. His departure meant that he missed Salford's biggest match to date, when they played the touring Maori side in March 1889, although he did play against them for Lancashire. In an about-turn, he was back at Salford the next season to the relief, no doubt, of the committee. This time he stayed at Salford long enough to enjoy the success of winning the first Lancashire Club Championship, in 1892/93. In August 1894, he joined Radcliffe for a third time, not to return.

Steve Kerry

Scrum-half/stand-off half/wing three-quarter, 1988-1992

Birthplace: Prescot
Signed from: Preston Grasshoppers RU

Debut: 11 December 1988 v. Bradford Northern (home)
Final match: 22 March 1992 v. Wigan (away)

Appearances: 105 (includes 8 as substitute)
Tries: 47
Goals: 318
Points: 812

Representative honours: Lancashire
Club honours: Second Division Championship 1990/91, Second Division Premiership 1991

Steve Kerry experienced the highs and lows in less than four seasons at Salford. In 1990/91, he had a spectacular season as Salford ran away with the Second Division Championship, completing the 'double' at Old Trafford in the Second Division Premiership final against Halifax. Salford won 27-20 and Kerry capped a wonderful season, winning the Tom Bergin Trophy as the outstanding player. He ended the campaign with a personal tally of 177 goals, and only David Watkins, on two occasions, could claim a better return. His 20 tries boosted his points total for the season to 427 and, again, only the mercurial Watkins had ever bettered that figure.

Salford should have realised they was getting a points machine when Kevin Ashcroft signed him from Preston Grasshoppers in December 1988 when he was twenty-two. At the time, he was the season's leading club point scorer in English Rugby Union. He finished his first campaign as the Reds' top goalscorer, albeit with just 30. It was the first of three consecutive seasons where Kerry would head both goal and point charts at The Willows. There was some uncertainty as to his best position in the first two seasons,

playing at stand-off, wing and centre, but finally settling into the scrum-half berth. His first match in that role was on 19 August 1990, at Rochdale Hornets in a Lancashire Cup tie. Salford won 41-12 and it was the first step to reaching the final, eventually losing heroically against Widnes 24-18 at Wigan.

Kerry was rewarded for his exploits with selection for Lancashire in the match against Yorkshire at the start of the following season (1991/92). Picked as a substitute, he replaced Bobbie Goulding in the seventy-fifth minute. However, from that point on, it all went wrong for Kerry. Salford were back in the First Division and coach Kevin Tamati, who had replaced Ashcroft in 1989, did not favour the lightweight scrum-half for the rigours of the top-flight competition. He played little during 1991/92, although he appeared in the last four games of the season, all on the wing. They were his final appearances for Salford. He was transferred to Oldham in October 1992 and later to Huddersfield in October 1994, for whom he appeared in another Second Division Premiership final, in the 1995 defeat against Keighley.

Tom King

Forward, 1889-1897

Birthplace: Manchester
Signed from: unknown

Debut: 16 February 1889 v. Liverpool (away)
Final match: 3 April 1897 v. Stockport (away)

Appearances: 221
Tries: 18
Goals: 15

Representative honours: Lancashire RU
Club honours: Lancashire RU Club Championship 1892/93

After joining Salford in February 1889, Thomas King had quite a busy start to his career. In only his fifth match, in March, he was playing in front of a 10,000 crowd at New Barnes as Salford took on the Maori touring team. Later in the year he received an invitation for the Lancashire county trial matches, played in October and November at Whalley Range. He lined up with the 'Whites' against the 'Stripes', a match convened for players with no previous county experience. King was one of the players selected after the game to go forward to the final trial, playing for the 'Possibles' in opposition to the 'Probables'. He failed to get through that stage into the county side but, nonetheless, his name had come to the fore and he eventually made his Lancashire debut in October 1892, in the match with Westmoreland. Over the next two years, he appeared in ten county fixtures for Lancashire.

In the 1892/93 season, he was a member of the Salford team that won the Lancashire Club Championship, playing in all but one of the league fixtures. In the following campaign, he took over the goal kicking duties, his 12 conversions making him the leading club goalscorer for that season. It was all to no avail, however, as Salford slipped to sixth in the Lancashire table, Oldham taking their crown. King made 207 appearances for Salford before they resigned from the Rugby Football Union in 1896, all of them in the pack, with the exception of two appearances on the wing in November 1895. He played in the club's first match under the Northern Union, a friendly against Tyldesley in April 1896, in the unfamiliar role of centre three-quarter. His last competitive match for Salford was in a Challenge Cup third round tie at Stockport, the Cheshire side winning 8-0. Following that, he took part in three end-of-season friendly games, the last of which was against Rochdale St Clements on 24 April 1897, before announcing his retirement.

After he finished as a player, he retained his association with the club by serving in various capacities, including having a seat on the executive committee for the 'Salford Football Club Bazaar' in 1903, designed to raise funds for the new ground at The Willows. He also joined the official list of Northern Union referees.

Harry Launce
Full-back, 1911-1920

Birthplace: Devonport
Signed from: Camborne RU

Debut: 2 September 1911 v. Rochdale Hornets (home)
Final match: 11 December 1920 v. Hull Kingston Rovers (home)

Appearances: 263 (includes 87 in wartime)
Tries: 3 (includes 1 in wartime)
Goals: 25 (includes 10 in wartime)
Points: 59 (includes 23 in wartime)

Representative honours: Cornwall RU
Club honours: Rugby League Championship 1913/14

The signature of William Henry (Harry) Launce in August 1911 ended a search by Salford that had covered the length and breadth of the country. Since Dan Smith had finished in 1904, several players had been tried at what had become a problematic full-back role for the club, including the dynamic half-back Dai John, but none gave the comfort and security that Smith had.

The arrival of the twenty-three-year-old from the Cornish League champions Camborne was announced by Salford with some relief. Only 5 ft 6 in and born in Devon, he had qualified, through his club rugby, to represent the county of Cornwall at Rugby Union. His first match for Salford though, against Rochdale Hornets, was followed with some concern by the media. One report said: 'Launce will want much experience before he comes up to the requirement of a Northern Union full-back'. The Salford club kept faith and, apart from an injury spell, he was picked for all the club matches during his first season. In only his tenth match, in December, he played for the Reds against the Australians, when the tourists won 6-3. Salford's patience with their new defender paid off and, at the end of the season, the same writer noted:

'Launce is a much improved exponent of full-back play and has shown gradual improvement over the season'.

Launce was virtually ever present at full-back from then on, and even through the wartime matches of 1915 to 1918, he was nearly always on view, becoming as steady as the proverbial rock at the back. Only two of his 263 matches were not played at full-back, when he filled in at three-quarter. As fate would have it, a high percentage of his time at Salford was disrupted by the activities of the First World War, a period when he played almost a third of his games for the Reds. In January 1915 he was suspended with the remainder of the Salford first team for refusing to make concessions in his match fees for the Relief Fund.

His biggest reward at Salford was having a place in the team that gained the marvellous championship final victory over Huddersfield in 1914 although, frustratingly for Launce, he suffered a second-half rib injury and had to leave the game for a period. On a day for heroes, he returned to make a vital last-ditch tackle, before being forced to retire once more.

Mark Lee
Hooker/scrum-half, 1990-2000

Birthplace: St Helens
Signed from: St Helens

Debut: 14 January 1990 v. Wakefield Trinity (away)
Final match: 8 August 2000 substitute v. Warrington (away)

Appearances: 254 (includes 17 as substitute)
Tries: 34
Goals: 34
Points: 170

Representative honours: none
Club honours: Second Division Championship 1990/91, First Division Championship 1996, Centenary First Division Championship 1995/96, Second Division Premiership 1991, Divisional Premiership 1996

When Mark Lee arrived from St Helens for a £15,000 transfer fee in January 1990, it is doubtful that Salford chairman John Wilkinson realised what a wonderful investment he had made. The virtually unknown hooker turned into one of the best clubmen seen at The Willows, giving his best in over 250 games during a period of eleven years. Lee had joined his town team St Helens from their Colts side in 1985, having earlier played for the local Hare and Hounds club. As a ten-year-old, he had captained St Helens schoolboys against Wakefield at Wembley in 1979. First-team opportunities were rare at Knowsley Road and he managed only seven games, but there were no such qualms in the Salford camp, as he became first choice hooker from the moment he signed.

It did not take too long before he showed his other attribute – that of a drop-goal king! He registered the first of 34 for the Reds (he also got one with St Helens) in the second round Challenge Cup tie against Oldham on 11 February 1990. The following season he scored 10 in a campaign that brought the Second Division Championship and Premiership home and, naturally, he scored a 'trademark' drop-goal in the Premiership final against Halifax at Old Trafford. Earlier in that season, he played in the Lancashire Cup final when the Reds lost to Widnes 24-18.

For the abbreviated 1995/96 season (due to the impending change to a summer schedule) he was given a new challenge by coach Andy Gregory when handed the scrum-half jersey. An unlikely move proved a big success and Lee was an inspirational figure in the Salford side as both playmaker and positional kicker. The Centenary First Division Championship of that season was won, a feat matched when the side added the inaugural summertime First Division title of 1996. That 1996 success brought promotion to the SuperLeague competition and the season was climaxed by a return to Old Trafford for the Premiership final, Lee playing his part in the convincing 19-6 win over Keighley.

Appropriately, Lee's last full match was against his former club at St Helens on 21 May 2000, his final appearance being at Warrington in August 2000 when he was a sixty-fifth minute replacement for Matthew Leigh. He received a club record £40,000 benefit in 2000. He began 2001 with Charley Lynx, before returning to join Salford's coaching staff.

Jimmy Lomas

Centre three-quarter/stand-off half, 1901-1910, 1917, 1923

Birthplace: Maryport
Signed from: Bramley

Debut: 21 September 1901 v. Leigh (away)
Final match: 29 September 1923 v. Wakefield Trinity (away)

Appearances: 315 (includes 3 in wartime)
Tries: 212 (includes 2 in wartime)
Goals: 471 (includes 1 in wartime)
Points: 1578 (includes 8 in wartime)

Representative honours: Tourist 1910 (tour captain), Great Britain, England, Cumberland, Lancashire
Club honours: Rugby League Championship 1910/11 (Oldham)

James (Jimmy) Lomas is a legend, not only at Salford, but throughout the world of Rugby League. It took the princely sum of £100 to sign the centre or stand-off from Bramley in August 1901, the first three-figure transfer fee in the game – although he was initially 'poached' by Salford! Born in Maryport, Cumberland, in August 1879, he played for the local team, but in the summer of 1900 was enticed to Bramley. During 1900/01, he played for the Leeds-based side 31 times before he was spirited away to Salford. The Reds got away with it because Bramley was then associated with the Yorkshire Senior Competition, then in dispute with the new Northern Rugby League, of which Salford were members. The rival organisations patched up their differences the following year and the record 'transfer' fee determined by tribunal. It was a figure that stood until 1911, when Oldham paid Salford £300 for Lomas' services.

The Rugby League fraternity remember him best as the first tour captain to the Antipodes in 1910. He had already appeared for Great Britain in the Second Test match against the first Australian tourists at Newcastle-upon-Tyne in 1909. Although it

was his debut, he was the team captain and it is an amazing fact that on each of the 8 occasions that he played for Great Britain he led the team. On tour, the First Test match in the Sydney Royal Agricultural Ground was preceded by a goal-kicking contest between the two captains; Lomas and Australia's Dally Messenger. In front of 42,000 people – a new Rugby League record – Lomas won and then added another goal as his team triumphed in that opening Test 27-10 on the way to a series win. He contributed a try and six goals as New Zealand were trounced 52-20 in a one-off Test in Auckland.

Lomas' first international appearance had been for England against the Other Nationalities team at Wigan in April 1904 – the first international match played. Lomas was selected for the English side 13 times during his career. Being on the Salford register qualified him to represent Lancashire and, following a county trial match at Widnes, he made his debut, ironically, against his native Cumberland at Millom in January 1903. From then, until February 1906, he turned out for the Lancastrians nine times. In September 1906 though, he withdrew from the Lancashire trials, declaring his intention to play for his county of origin, his first outing being the following month against Lancashire! His last match for Cumberland – and his last representative match of any description – was in December 1912, after eleven appearances.

At Salford, where he was team captain from 1902 until 1910, Lomas was a phenomenon and he dominated the British game in a way no one had ever done before him. Although only 5 ft 7 in tall, he weighed over 13 stone and was extremely difficult to stop, often brushing would-be tacklers to one side. He was a dominating figure whenever he played, with one journalist claiming: 'When Lomas was on the field you never noticed anybody else!'

In the nine full seasons that he played for Salford, he was the club's leading try scorer, goalscorer and point scorer each time. He broke the club goal record in his first campaign with 53, and the points record with 172, figures that seem modest by today's standards, but the previous records were 26 and 107 respectively. He broke both records twice more, setting the standard at 82 goals and 266 points in 1906/07 – statistics that would stand for twenty-four years. In that same season, his 34-try total was also a new high for the club, and an achievement that nobody could replicate until Bob Brown's exploits of 1933/34. He was the leading point scorer in the Rugby League in seven seasons and set a new record in three of those. He was the sport's top marksman three times, and his 86 in 1906/07 (which included representative matches) was a new Rugby League landmark. On 2 March 1907, he scored 39 points (5 tries, 12 goals) against Liverpool City, a record haul for a championship fixture until Dean Marwood scored 42 for Workington Town in 1992.

It seemed as though Lomas could do no wrong, but one thing was missing in his glittering career. In spite of the fact that he was with a more-than-useful side at Salford, club honours eluded him. With Salford, he played in four finals but, not only did they fail to win any of them, they also failed to score a point! Three were Challenge Cup finals; Broughton Rangers (25-0 in 1902), Halifax

THE LOMAS TOUCH

ONCE UPON A TIME, A GREAT BIG HE-MAN NAMED JIMMY LOMAS USED TO TUCK A RUGBY BALL UNDER HIS LEFT ARM, PUSH OUT HIS IRON RIGHT, & WIN GAMES FOR SALFORD.

As this caricature clearly illustrates, Jimmy Lomas was a legendary figure during his own lifetime.

(7-0 in 1903) and Bradford (5-0 in 1906). The other was a championship decider against Bradford in 1904, the score-line being 5-0.

It was a problem resolved after transferring to Oldham in January 1911, playing his final match for Salford on New Year's Eve 1910, against Barrow. His first big date with Oldham happened at the conclusion of that first season when he played in the championship final against Wigan. Oldham won 20-7 and Lomas contributed two tries and four goals – he had a winner's medal at last! He was less successful in his two other finals for Oldham, losing to Rochdale Hornets in the 1911 Lancashire Cup final and Dewsbury in the 1912 Challenge Cup final. In three seasons, he took part in 78 matches for Oldham, moving to York in 1913, playing a further 52 games before retiring. He made two unexpected comebacks for Salford, the first for three wartime games in April 1917. He then took over as reserve team coach in August 1922 and was tempted to help out during 1923, playing six times in February and March and twice more in September, when he was forty-four.

Tom McKinney
Hooker, 1949-1954

Birthplace: Ballymena, Antrim
Signed from: Jed-Forest RU

Debut: 26 November 1949 v. Hunslet (home)
Final match: 27 November 1954 v. Leigh (home)

Appearances: 148
Tries: 0
Goals: 4
Points: 8

Representative honours: Tourist 1954, Great Britain, Great Britain World Cup Squad 1957, Other Nationalities
Club honours: Rugby League Championship 1954/55 (Warrington) and 1958/59 (St Helens), ITV Floodlit Cup 1955 (Warrington)

Although originating from Ireland, hooker Tom McKinney was a product of Scottish Rugby Union, and selected for the Scotland trials until his ancestry was realised. Joining Salford in November 1949, he competed with George Curran for the hooking role and established the position as his own in 1950/51.

He soon gained the attention of the international selectors. His first international match was for the Other Nationalities against England at Wigan in April 1951 and he made eight appearances altogether, sharing in two European Championship successes, in 1952/53 and 1955/56. His Great Britain debut was also in 1951, playing against New Zealand in the Third Test at Headingley in December. The following year, he played in two Tests against the 1952 Kangaroos. Selected for the 1954 tour party Down Under, he played in 22 of the tour matches including all three Tests against Australia as Britain retained the 'Ashes'. He also appeared in the deciding Third Test against New Zealand – won 12-6 by the tourists.

After he returned from the tour, he played just 12 matches for Salford before transferring to Warrington in January 1955. His international career continued, and he played in the three-match series against the touring Kiwis in 1955. In January 1957, he moved to St Helens and, later that year, was with the Great Britain World Cup squad in Australia, playing in one match – against New Zealand in Sydney. It was his sixteenth, and final, appearance for Great Britain. He did play in the 1958 tour trials but failed to gain selection. Other representative honours were playing for the British Empire XIII against New Zealand in 1952 (at Chelsea's Stamford Bridge), the Combined Nations against France at Lyon in 1954 (for the twentieth anniversary of French Rugby League), and three times for a British XIII against a French XIII in 1957 – one match in New Zealand and two in South Africa.

On the domestic front, McKinney appeared in two victorious championship finals with Warrington in 1955 (7-3 over Oldham at Maine Road) and St Helens in 1959 (44-22 against Hunslet at Odsal). He also reached two Lancashire Cup finals with St Helens in 1958 and 1959, but both were lost. His other club success was in the experimental ITV floodlit competition played in London in 1955, Warrington beating Leigh 43-18 in the final.

David Major

Second row forward/prop forward, 1979-1989

Birthplace: Warrington
Signed from: Crosfields ARL (Warrington)

Debut: 30 November 1979 substitute v. St Helens (away)
Final match: 2 April 1989 substitute v. Halifax (home)

Appearances: 221 (includes 70 as substitute)
Tries: 10
Goals: 0
Points: 39

Representative honours: none
Club honours: none

When David Major joined Salford in November 1979, he came as a nineteen-year-old with a fine pedigree. Having represented Great Britain under-18s, Lancashire under-18s, Lancashire under-19s and Lancashire schoolboys, the Reds – who were coached by Alex Murphy at that time – faced a lot of competition to obtain his signature. After making his first appearance as a substitute for Harold Henney in a BBC2 Floodlit Cup-tie defeat at St Helens, he had four more substitute outings before his first start, in the second row at Wakefield Trinity on 13 April 1980.

In his second term with Salford in 1980/81 he became a regular member of the team, appearing in 34 matches. His most memorable match that season had been partnering Henney and Stewart Williams in an all-action back-row when Widnes were beaten 26-10 in one of the upsets of the season on their Naughton Park ground. During an interview at the end of that campaign, he said: 'I will try to go all out next season and really establish myself in the first team. My ambition is to get to Wembley like my father did.' His father, Harry, had been an excellent forward for Oldham, Warrington and Wigan, and Major

junior considered him as one of the biggest influences on his rugby career. 'He gives me plenty of good advice' he said, 'For instance, he helped me when I switched to centre recently. When he was at Warrington he played centre to Brian Bevan.'

In fact that move to the centre, early in 1981, was a short-lived affair. He found himself back amongst the forwards the following season, although it was a delayed start, Major not appearing until November, as the result of a groin injury. He was unable to claim any trophies whilst at The Willows, but played his part in the promotion campaigns of 1982/83 and 1984/85 and appeared in the 1988 Challenge Cup semi-final against Wigan at Bolton Wanderer's former Burnden Park, losing 34-4. In April 1984, he was in the Salford team that played in Perpignan against Catalan to celebrate fifty years of Rugby League in France. Although his last official game for Salford occurred in April 1989 against Halifax, he turned out in his testimonial match against Oldham on 27 August 1989, played as part of his benefit year.

William Manwaring
Full-back, 1886-1897

Birthplace: Salford
Signed from: Broughton (Salford)

Debut: 18 September 1886 v. Warrington (home)
Final match: 3 April 1897 v. Stockport (away)

Appearances: 300
Tries: 3
Goals: 44

Representative honours: Lancashire RU
Club honours: Lancashire RU Club Championship 1892/93

William Manwaring was, at 5 ft 5 in, small in stature and affectionately referred to as 'Little Manwaring'. He was to reign supreme, however, as the Salford full-back during his eleven seasons at the club. In total, he played 276 times for Salford under Rugby Union rules – a record during their time as members of that code. He started his career as a sixteen-year-old with a junior club, known as The Alma, based in Pendleton. Manwaring played one season for them at full-back and then 'retired'. Eventually, he was tempted back playing for Broughton in their three-quarter line. In 1886, he joined Salford with the intention of playing in their line but, as there was no vacancy, he was tried at full-back.

It was not until his seventy-third match for Salford that he registered his first points for the club, a match-winning drop-goal at home to Millom in January 1889. Two months later, he took part in Salford's historic match against the Maori tourists on 16 March at New Barnes, when it was reported: 'He played one of the greatest games of his career'. Five days earlier, he had met the same opposition when representing a Manchester XV.

In the following season, Manwaring received his first calling from Lancashire when he travelled to Weston-super-Mare to face Somerset on 11 January 1890. A fortnight later, he had to go to the opposite end of the country to face Durham in Hartlepool! He played four matches for the county that season, but did not represent them again until November 1895, against Cheshire. Played at Swinton, it was the first by the Lancashire RU after the formation of the Northern Union. All told, Manwaring represented Lancashire on nine occasions.

He won his only club honour as a member of the Salford team that were the first Lancashire champions in 1892/93, playing in 7 of the 15 championship fixtures. He became captain in the 1895/96 season, a position he retained after they joined the Northern Union in 1896. He played 24 games under the auspices of the Northern Union, his last official match being a Challenge Cup tie at Stockport on 3 April 1897. Following that, he played in five end-of-season friendly games, the last at home to Barton on 28 April 1897, converting a try in an 11-9 win before announcing his retirement.

Birthplace: Gloucester
Signed from: Ebbw Vale RU

Debut: 29 August 1925 v. Hull (home)
Final match: 30 September 1933 v. St Helens (away)

Appearances: 260
Tries: 32
Goals: 25
Points: 146

Representative honours: Glamorgan and Monmouthshire
Club honours: Lancashire Cup 1931, Lancashire League Championship 1932/33

Reginald Meek joined Salford in 1925, at a time when the club was usually consigned to the lower third of the table. He played his first few seasons at scrum-half, partnering in succession the evergreen Sandy Hurst, Tommy Mannion, Jimmy Lindley and, from 1928, Eddie Matthews, who had arrived from the Neath Rugby Union club as one of Lance Todd's first signings. The two became the regular combination during Todd's first two seasons at The Willows and they led the Reds in their renaissance.

He appeared in his first final in 1929 – for the Lancashire Cup – when, as partner to recent signing Sammy Miller, he gave everything in an attempt to win his first award. According to the press: 'Meek played heroically, he was here, there and everywhere'. Sadly, that day had ended in disappointment. The signing of another scrum-half in Billy Watkins from Aberavon Rugby Union in 1931 saw Meek switched to out-half and it was in that position that he secured his first honour with the club. The pair lined up together in the successful Lancashire Cup final bid of 1931 against Swinton, for what was Meek's happiest day in Rugby League.

Although he was born in the county town of Gloucestershire, he represented Glamorgan and Monmouthshire in the county championship on two occasions, possibly because he had learnt his trade in Welsh Rugby Union. He made his debut with them against Lancashire at Pontypridd in November 1927, playing at scrum-half in a 12-7 win. The second of his matches – against the same county – was in November 1930 at The Willows. Playing again at scrum-half, he finished on the winning side once more, this time by 14-10. He also represented Salford on two occasions against touring teams. In November 1926, he scored a try in the 18-10 loss to New Zealand and was in the team beaten 21-5 by the Australians in January 1930. By 1932/33, as the Watkins-Emlyn Jenkins era began, he found himself very much on the fringe of the Salford team, although he did play in six of the matches that secured the club's first Lancashire League Championship title that season. In December 1933, he transferred to Keighley, playing in 91 matches for them before retiring from the game in 1936.

Bernard Mesley

Wing three-quarter/centre three-quarter, 1908-1916

Birthplace: Twickenham
Signed from: Twickenham RU

Debut: 26 September 1908 v. Broughton Rangers (away)
Final match: 7 October 1916 (wartime match) v. Broughton Rangers (home)

Appearances: 214 (includes 1 in wartime)
Tries: 87 (includes 1 in wartime)
Goals: 171
Points: 603 (includes 3 in wartime)

Representative honours: Middlesex RU
Club honours: Rugby League Championship 1913/14

The old adage 'Cometh the hour, cometh the man' was never truer than on that windswept Saturday afternoon at Headingley on 25 April 1914, the man in question being Salford wing three-quarter, Bernard Mesley. The Reds were in their first championship final, opposing an all-conquering Huddersfield outfit that had dominated the pre-First World War era. In blustery conditions, Salford had managed to claw back from an early Huddersfield try when Reds forward Charlie Rees touched down in the corner. With scoring opportunities limited, it was down to Mesley to attempt the difficult conversion from the touchline. Many a player would have wilted under the pressure but the ball sailed between the uprights despite the gale force wind, and the Salford fans were in ecstasy. It was the final score of the match and Mesley was the hero of the hour.

He was seen at Salford for the first time when invited to the pre-season trials for 1908/09, the press reporting that he 'was a clever centre three-quarter' and 'had shaped well'. Aged twenty-one at the time, he was with Twickenham Rugby Union club and had represented Middlesex County, the Civil Service and Oxford University, accompanying the latter to Paris the previous year to take on the University of France. Duly signed on 8 September, he made his debut in the club's fourth match of the season at Broughton Rangers. Three weeks later he was pitched against the touring Kangaroos and, with regular goal-kicker Jimmy Lomas unavailable, took over. Undaunted, he banged over two goals in a tight 9-9 draw.

Losing form, he returned home after the 1910/11 season but, after a change of heart, reappeared in mid-September during 1911/12. He quickly found his old sparkle and it was reported that 'his work is reminiscent of his early association with the club'. He did not look back, becoming the regular right wing three-quarter from 1911/12 and taking over the responsibility for place kicks after Lomas' departure to Oldham. For the next four seasons, he was the club's top goal and point scorer and leading try scorer in 1912/13 (20) and 1914/15 (8). He gained no representative honours but did meet the Australians for a second time in Salford colours during December 1911, scoring the only try in a 6-3 defeat. After leaving Salford, he played for the Army, a reported return for 1920/21 not materialising.

Alf Middleton

Second row forward, 1928-1936

Birthplace: Nuneaton
Signed from: Coventry RU

Debut: 10 November 1928 v. Widnes (away)
Final match: 28 March 1936 v. Castleford (away)

Appearances: 285
Tries: 67
Goals: 25
Points: 251

Representative honours: Great Britain, England, Warwickshire RU
Club honours: Rugby League Championship 1932/33, Lancashire Cup 1931, 1934 and 1935, Lancashire League Championship 1932/33, 1933/34 and 1934/35

Alf Middleton was one of Lance Todd's earliest signings in October 1928 and became an integral part of the rise of the great Salford team of that era. Todd had a lot of respect for the leadership qualities of the strong, quick second-rower, and Middleton took over the captaincy of the team from Fergie Southward. In the following years, he formed a strong back row with Aubrey Casewell and Jack Feetham, becoming one of the original Red Devils in the club's historic tour of France in 1934.

In November 1929, he led Salford to their first Lancashire Cup final against Warrington but lost 15-2, on the only occasion Middleton captained the team in a final. In September 1931, he resigned from the role and Billy Williams took over. Two months later, in November 1931, Salford was back in the Lancashire Cup final and Middleton shared in the 10-8 victory over Swinton. The following season, Middleton enjoyed his biggest moment with the Reds when the championship decider was won, Swinton again the victims, this time by 15-5. He was also in the team which lost in the following season's championship final, but enjoyed further success with the lifting, once more, of the Lancashire Cup in 1934 and 1935, both times defeating Wigan in the final.

He had quickly drawn the attention of the international selectors when in October 1929 – just one year after turning professional – he was in the Great Britain side to meet the Australians in the First Test at Craven Park, Hull. The Aussies won 31-8 and Middleton was one of the scapegoats from that result, never representing Britain again. He did play for England, although, again, it was to be a solitary outing when, in March 1931, he played in the 23-18 victory over Wales at Huddersfield. His one other representative game was with the Rugby League XIII who took on the touring French side Lyon-Villeurbanne at York in September 1935, winning 23-19. At the beginning of the 1936/37 season it was announced in the local paper: 'Middleton is still finding all his time occupied with his (boarding house) business in Blackpool and it is unlikely that he will re-sign, at least for some time yet'. In fact, he had played his last match for Salford and retired prematurely.

87

Frank Miles

Wing three-quarter, 1889-1894, 1897-1899

Birthplace: Eccles, near Salford
Signed from: Barton (Eccles)

Debut: 14 September 1889 v. Rochdale Hornets (home)
Final match: 18 February 1899 v. Oldham (away)

Appearances: 180
Tries: 128
Goals: 5

Representative honours: Lancashire RU
Club honours: Lancashire RU Club Championship 1892/93

Frank Miles could lay claim to being Salford's first star; an exciting wing three-quarter guaranteed to attract the supporters to any ground. Although in his teens, he found himself in the first team when Jack Anderton left the club, unexpectedly, in 1889. After an uncertain start, he quickly gained confidence, bringing the comment from James Higson that he was 'one of the most brilliant players the club has ever produced'. One journalist wrote that he ran 'with a swiftness that defied pursuit'. Certainly, his speed and elusiveness contrasted to the direct running style of Anderton.

His exploits were many and varied. He led the club try lists for five consecutive seasons and twice set a new club record for tries in a season. His 27 in 1890/91 was extraordinary for that time and, against Oldham junior side Lees in March 1898, he set a club record with 6 touchdowns. That figure has not been beaten, although it has been equalled twice. In a match against Runcorn in February 1890, he scored three tries in only five minutes, a feat repeated by David Watkins in 1972. Miles was also the first successful captain of Salford when the Lancashire Club Championship was secured in 1892/93.

Born in nearby Eccles in 1871, he started his rugby career at fifteen, playing in the three-quarters for Brackley Juniors. After two seasons, he went to Barton where he played for one and a half seasons, before being injured midway through 1888/89. He did not play for Barton again, choosing instead to play in Salford's pre-season trials for 1889/90. Anticipating a place with the reserves, he suddenly found himself promoted due to Anderton's departure. His Lancashire debut came later that first season in February, at Whitehaven against Cumberland. Over the next two years, he would play 6 times for the county.

His first spell at Salford ended on 13 October 1894, in a Lancashire Club Championship match against Swinton. After this match, Salford were suspended for ten weeks for alleged player payments and Miles did not return, having been suspended himself by the Lancashire committee for accepting payment from Wigan to play for them. He returned to Salford after they joined the Northern Union, reappearing against Widnes on 23 January 1897 and playing 23 times over the next two years.

Sammy Miller

Centre three-quarter/stand-off half, 1929-1945

Birthplace: Aspatria, Cumberland
Signed from: Blaydon-on-Tyne RU

Debut: 18 November 1929 v. Swinton (away)
Final match: 22 December 1945 v. Broughton Rangers (away)

Appearances: 312
Tries: 81
Goals: 57
Points: 357

Representative honours: Cumberland, Northumberland RU
Club honours: Rugby League Championship 1932/33, 1936/37, 1938/39 and 1941/42 (Dewsbury), Lancashire Cup 1931, 1934, 1935 and 1936, Lancashire League Championship 1932/33, 1933/34, 1934/35, 1936/37 and 1938/39

Samuel Edward 'Sammy' Miller had a baptism of fire for Salford in November 1929, making his debut at stand-off in a Lancashire Cup semi-final replay at Swinton, which ended scoreless. His next match was two days later, in the second replay played on neutral territory at Broughton Rangers ground, Salford winning 8-0. To complete an amazing treble he played in the final three days later against Warrington at Wigan. Small wonder that Salford lost 15-2 in the club's first major final since 1914.

Although a Cumbrian, Miller had represented Northumberland at Rugby Union, qualifying as a member of the Blaydon-on-Tyne club, before joining Salford in August 1929. He became something of a utility back but as Tom Bergin, writing in the programme for Miller's testimonial match in 1947 (shared with Bert Day and Jack Feetham), said: 'Miller was, without doubt, one of the finest all-rounders to play for the club and he filled the centre, half-back and full-back berths with equal distinction. It is no secret that many clubs were anxious to obtain his transfer, but his heart was with the Reds. His nickname might well have been 'Consistency' for, no matter in which position

he played, he gave a sound display. His greatest playing qualities were his imperturbability and his rock-like defence.'

The biggest disappointment of his career was being a non-playing reserve when Salford met Barrow at Wembley in 1938, although he was in the 1939 side that lost to Halifax. Nonetheless, he shared in many of the greatest moments, including the championship final victories over Swinton in 1933 and Castleford in 1939. He missed out on the 1937 final win over Warrington but still got his medal. After his unusual start with Salford in the 1929 Lancashire Cup, he appeared in four more finals, all ending in victories for the Reds. His first match for Cumberland was on 20 September 1930 against Yorkshire at Whitehaven. He was to play eighteen times for them and shared in three county championship wins. He also represented a Northern Rugby League XIII against Cote Basque of France at Oldham in October 1936. During the Second World War he won another championship medal, guesting for Dewsbury in their 1942 win over Bradford Northern at Headingley. After the war, he played in four more matches for Salford before retiring.

Dai Moses
Loose forward/second row forward/prop forward, 1945-1958

Birthplace: Nanty Moel, Bridgend
Signed from: Maesteg RU

Debut: 8 December 1945 v. Wigan (away)
Final match: 11 February 1958 v. Keighley (away)

Appearances: 328
Tries: 29
Goals: 4
Points: 95

Representative honours: none
Club honours: none

Dai Moses was one of the most committed forwards ever to play for Salford. Starting his career in the back row, he matured into an uncompromising prop forward. Whilst the Reds supporters loved him, he was hated by opposing fans. Cries of 'Dirty Moses!' were often heard on the terraces. He sustained many injuries over the years, breaking most of his fingers, his nose eight times and his collar bone. He also had three cartilage operations and even had a knee-cap removed. That was in addition to the usual occupational hazard of losing teeth!

He joined Salford from Maesteg in 1945. 'Cyril Braund was Salford's manager and he was from Bridgend' said Moses. 'An old school friend of mine was scouting for him in the area, and he recommended me to the club.' His debut at Wigan saw him at loose-foward, a position he occupied for several seasons, moving into the second row from 1949 and up to prop in 1956. His brother, Glyn, joined him at Salford in 1948. A centre-cum-full-back, he stayed for three seasons before moving on to St Helens.

In his first season, Moses made such an impact that he was in contention for the 1946 tour, but injured both ankles while training

with the squad at Leeds. That was the closest he ever got to representative honours in Rugby League, although he did turn out for a Welsh XIII in March 1959 against France at Toulouse – but that match did not carry full international status.

He spent the best part of eleven seasons with Salford, joining Swinton for £500 in 1958. 'Gus Risman had taken over as the coach and I did not figure in his plans. When Cliff Evans came to see me and said he thought I could do a good job for Swinton, I jumped at the chance.' Evans' judgment was sound and Moses played an important part as pack leader in Swinton's revival at that time. In 1960, he reached his only cup final, playing for the Lions against St Helens in the Lancashire Cup decider at Wigan. A crowd of 31,755 saw the Saints carry the day 15-9. In March 1961 he ended his playing days with his ninetieth appearance for the Lions, at Blackpool. When he retired, he took to coaching at Swinton, returning to Salford in 1969 to join the coaching staff for the Salford Colts side. He later became head groundsman at The Willows.

Jack Muir

Second row forward/prop forward, 1920-1933

Birthplace: Salford
Signed from: Manchester district ARL

Debut: 16 October 1920 v. Rochdale Hornets (away)
Final match: 16 September 1933 v. Leigh (away)

Appearances: 338
Tries: 14
Goals: 0
Points: 42

Representative honours: none
Club honours: none

John (Jack) Muir was seen in Salford colours for the first time at Rochdale Hornets ground in a first round Lancashire Cup tie during October 1920, when he was promoted from the reserves and, according to the match report, 'played a hard game'. The Hornets won 11-5, a result hardly unexpected as it was the club's seventh defeat from seven played and they finished with three wins all season. The young back row forward, signed in September 1920, had certainly joined a club that was in the middle of strife but, undeterred, he established himself in the pack, playing in twenty matches before the season closed. He continued to give good service, averaging twenty-seven matches a campaign over the next eight seasons, prior to Lance Todd's arrival in the summer of 1928.

Muir became one of the cornerstones of Todd's pack during the New Zealander's first three seasons in charge. Todd moved him from the second row to blind-side prop, the other prop being a youthful Billy Williams. Muir adapted to the demanding role with great success and was virtually ever-present. Although still not winning trophies, Muir found himself thrust into the limelight and appeared in championship semi-finals in both

1929 and 1930. Salford was on the verge of greatness, but on those occasions Huddersfield twice got the better of the Reds at their Fartown enclosure. One final reached by Muir, however, was for the 1929 Lancashire Cup against Warrington at Wigan's Central Park. Muir played his heart out at prop as he chased his first medal, one scribe commenting that 'Muir was outstanding and in fact one of the best men on the side'. It was all to no avail as Salford lost 15-2, hardly surprising as, for Muir and his colleagues, it was their fifth game in ten days courtesy of two energy-sapping semi-final replays with Swinton.

The arrival of Joe Bradbury at prop, combined with reaching the veteran stage himself, cost him his place in 1931/32, Muir appearing just three times, including two at the end of season in place of Billy Williams (who had set off for the 1932 tour). It was another seventeen months before his next, and final, match in a 28-20 win at Leigh. Although he missed representative honours, he faced three touring sides with Salford; the Australians in 1921 and 1930, and the New Zealanders in 1926.

Steve Nash
Scrum-half, 1975-1984

Birthplace: Featherstone
Signed from: Featherstone Rovers

Debut: 15 August 1975 v. Dewsbury (home)
Final match: 8 January 1984 v. Featherstone Rovers (away)

Appearances: 275
Tries: 31
Goals: 26
Points: 128

Representative honours: Tourist 1974 and 1979, Great Britain, Great Britain World Cup Squad 1972 and 1977, England, England World Cup Squad 1975, Yorkshire
Club honours: Rugby League Championship 1975/76, Rugby League Challenge Cup 1973 (Featherstone Rovers)

From early childhood, living in Post Office Road and overlooking the ground, the destiny of Steve Nash was surely to join the famous scrum-half factory of Featherstone Rovers. As he once explained: 'My lack of inches prevented me from being anything other than a half-back. Featherstone used to decide the stand-off and scrum-half positions by having both half backs race over 100 yards, the winner playing number six. Initially, I won the sprints and played most of my early games at stand-off. Then, I started coming second, and a scrum-half was born.' He was the proverbial seventh forward and loved nothing more than running at the opposition pack, whilst his tackling was as deadly as that of any half-back in the game.

Nash signed for the Rovers in 1967 and went to Wembley with them twice, hammering Bradford Northern in 1973 – when he won the Lance Todd trophy for his outstanding performance – and losing to Warrington in 1974. 'Losing at Wembley is the worst thing I have experienced in Rugby League. Within twelve months I had my happiest and saddest moments in the game – and both at Wembley!'

He joined Salford in August 1975 when, for the fourth consecutive time, Salford set a Rugby League transfer record, paying out £15,000. Featherstone had sold him to relieve a £7,000 overdraft, although Nash himself had become unsettled. He was an established Great Britain international, having played for the victorious 1972 World Cup team in France, and he had been a member of the 1974 tour party. Immediately before joining Salford, he was in Australasia with England's 1975 World Cup squad. Whilst at Salford he went on the 1979 tour and was in the Great Britain World Cup squad that travelled Down Under in 1977.

After several years in the wilderness, Nash returned to the international scene with England in March 1981 for the clash with Wales at Hull's Craven Park. It was his first international appearance in over two years. 'I thought my international career was over. When you have been out of the picture for a while you tend to get overlooked' he said. The crowning glory came when asked to lead the Great Britain team in the opening Test against the 1982 Australians in October. Before the match he said: 'Captaining Great Britain has to be the best moment of my career. I will not need to motivate the team.

Playing Australia in a Test match is motivation in itself'. The skill and power of that Kangaroo team revolutionised the game in this country and it was no surprise that Britain lost 40-4. Although he had played well in defeat, it was his final Test after appearing 25 times for Britain. He played 9 times in matches for England and 10 for Yorkshire.

Although his official Salford debut was against Dewsbury on 15 August 1975, he played his first match a week earlier, in a friendly fixture with St Helens. He contributed to Salford's championship success in his first season and appeared in the Lancashire Cup final in October against Widnes and the Premiership final with St Helens at the end of the campaign, both ending in defeat. Salford were coming to the end of a glorious period but Nash continued to give his total on-field commitment to the Reds' cause. After Salford suffered relegation in 1981, Nash – as team captain and assistant coach to Kevin Ashcroft – led the recovery that ended with promotion back into the top flight in 1983. His performance resulted in him receiving, at thirty-three, the Second Division Player of the Year trophy at the annual Man of Steel awards.

During the 1979 tour, he had suffered an eye injury, which got progressively worse and, in February 1983, he had an emergency operation on a torn retina. He returned to action but found the game was taking its toll on his body, particularly his knees. In the brochure for his testimonial in 1984, he announced: 'Since the start of my testimonial, I have decided to retire. It was a decision that was very hard to come to, but having played two pre-season games I realised that I could no longer do things on the rugby field that people have, over the years, expected from me. On top of that, two specialists and half a dozen friends can't all be wrong!' He joined Rochdale Hornets in September 1985 and appeared in 27 matches over two seasons before coaching the Mayfield amateur club. He had a brief spell in 1988/89 coaching Mansfield Marksman.

Helping to spread the word – Steve Nash sits on the bonnet of one of the Salford promotion vehicles.

Steve Nash keeps his eye on the ball for Great Britain. Paul Charlton looks on in the background.

Harold Osbaldestin

Full-back, 1931-1939

Birthplace: Wigan
Signed from: Dewsbury

Debut: 3 October 1931 v. Castleford (home)
Final match: 6 May 1939 v. Halifax (at Wembley)

Appearances: 271
Tries: 25
Goals: 48
Points: 171

Representative honours: Lancashire
Club honours: Rugby League Championship 1932/33, 1936/37 and 1938/39, Rugby League Challenge Cup 1938, Lancashire Cup 1931, 1934, 1935 and 1936, Lancashire League Championship 1932/33, 1933/34, 1934/35, 1936/37 and 1938/39

In an era of defensive-minded, kicking full-backs, Harold Osbaldestin was one of the finest attacking number ones in Rugby League during the 1930s. He may have recorded only 25 tries for Salford, but he popped up with the match-winner in critical situations on more than one occasion.

One of his finest days was in the 1936 Lancashire Cup final against Wigan at Wilderspool Stadium, Warrington. The game took place in atrocious conditions, with heavy rain and a driving wind throughout. Salford's tactic was to attack strongly in the opening quarter before the playing conditions worsened, and it paid off when Osbaldestin scored the only try of the match early on. One scribe described it as 'a masterpiece of opportunism and quick thinking'. The report went on to say: 'In addition to scoring the vital try of the game, he gave a performance he has never equalled. His try is worth a chapter on its own. Those three points haunted Wigan for the rest of the match.' Wigan never recovered and, in a low scoring final – dictated by the conditions – the Red Devils gained a narrow 5-2 victory thanks to Osbaldestin's alertness.

At the climax of that same season, league leaders Salford had a home tie in the semi-final of the top four championship play-off. The opposition was Liverpool Stanley, who had enjoyed their best season ever. There was a crowd of 14,000 in The Willows ground to see Salford record a 15-7 win on the way to taking that season's championship. A determined Stanley team made Salford fight all the way and things were looking uncomfortable for the home side until Osbaldestin struck. As one reporter said: 'The genius of Osbaldestin put Salford in the Rugby League Championship final. Twice the full-back joined in the attack, and each time a try was scored when it was badly needed. Things looked none too good for Salford but inspired action by Osbaldestin saved the situation. The full-back completely upset the Liverpool spotting system, which had held the Salford backs in a vice-like grip.'

Despite such plaudits, he found international honours beyond his reach in an era dominated by Jim Sullivan, but, justifiably, he did represent Lancashire on four occasions between 1933 and 1935.

Osbaldestin, nicknamed 'Ovaltine', had three seasons and 96 matches at Wigan Highfield before transferring to Dewsbury in

Harold Osbaldestin lines up with his illustrious colleagues prior to a cup replay at Hunslet in 1936. From left to right, back row: George Harris, Joe Bradbury, Bob Brown, Billy Williams, Jack Feetham, Bert Day, Alf Middleton, Osbaldestin, Barney Hudson. Front row: Alan Edwards, Billy Watkins, Gus Risman, Emlyn Jenkins.

1929, where he appeared 74 times. Salford snapped him up in 1931 but he did not get off to the best start as his debut was delayed by a month due to a shoulder injury in the pre-season trial game. He damaged it again in his seventh match and missing the rest of the season. His injury cost him a place in the Lancashire Cup final win of 1931, but he played sufficient games to collect his medal. He was back to fitness the next season, playing a part in the club's success during the years ahead and even scoring an unprecedented seven tries in the six matches played by Salford in their historic trip to France in 1934.

In Salford's return to Wembley in 1939, tragedy struck in the cup final with Halifax. Gus Risman recounted later: 'Osbaldestin leapt to catch a high ball. He caught it cleanly, landed perfectly and immediately turned to start his run. But he just sat down and looked stupefied. The attempt at a turn had wrenched his Achilles tendon.' Osbaldestin never played again.

A Salford public trial match at The Willows in August 1936; Harold Osbaldestin tackles Hayes.

Eric Prescott
Loose forward, 1972-1980, 1984

Birthplace: Widnes
Signed from: St Helens

Debut: 15 September 1972 v. Rochdale Hornets (home)
Final match: 26 December 1984 v. Swinton (away)

Appearances: 291 (includes 3 as substitute)
Tries: 51
Goals: 8
Points: 173

Representative honours: Lancashire
Club honours: Rugby League Championship 1969/70 (St Helens), 1973/74 and 1975/76, Rugby League Challenge Cup 1981 (Widnes), Premiership Trophy 1982 (Widnes) and 1983 (Widnes), Lancashire Cup 1972, BBC2 Floodlit Cup 1971/72 (St Helens) and 1974/75

Despite the big name signings, Salford were considered a vulnerable outfit in the early 1970s when it came to the big games, Alex Murphy famously calling them 'The Quality Street Gang'. When Eric Prescott arrived from St Helens in September 1972, it was to add steel to the pack. The tough-tackling Widnesian certainly achieved that, but it took a Rugby League record price of £13,500. Rated at the time as the finest forward prospect in the game at twenty-two, the St Helens chairman Harry Cooke said: 'We did not want to part with him. We realise he has a great future'.

St Helens signed him from the Widnes-based ICI Rugby Union team and his first success came on the wing in the 1970 championship final with Leeds, scoring two tries in a 24-12 win. With Saints, he won the Floodlit Cup in 1971 playing in the second row, having lost in the 1970 final and the 1970 Lancashire Cup final. His biggest blow came when a shoulder injury forced him to miss the 1972 Wembley final.

Claiming that he wanted to play loose forward, he went to Salford, who granted his wish and he became an established 'number thirteen'. He gained his first winner's medal with Salford in the 1972 Lancashire Cup final victory over Swinton, and played his part in the two championship wins of the 1970s as well as the 1974/75 Floodlit Cup win. He was in the losing final teams for the Lancashire Cup of 1973, 1974 and 1975, and the Premiership of 1976. He missed the 1973 John Player final defeat due to a dislocated shoulder.

After playing against St Helens on 19 September 1980, he transferred to Widnes for £22,000, having been unsettled for some time. For Prescott, the move paid dividends. With Widnes, he played in two Wembley finals – winning in 1981 – and two successful Premiership finals and was runner-up in two Lancashire Cup finals. He returned to Salford in January 1984 in exchange for prop John Wood, but due to suspension, his comeback was delayed until the home match with Hull on 11 March 1984.

He played eighteen times for Salford during 1984, joining Runcorn Highfield in 1985. Surprisingly, he gained no international honours, but he did play eleven times for Lancashire from 1970 until 1979.

Dave Preston

Stand-off half/scrum-half, 1902-1913

Birthplace: Salford
Signed from: Salford Trinity ARL

Debut: 13 December 1902 v. Oldham (away)
Final match: 15 November 1913 v. Barrow (away)

Appearances: 256
Tries: 41
Goals: 1
Points: 125

Representative honours: Lancashire
Club honours: none

Local boy David Preston, a graduate from the Manchester Rugby League, described in the press as a plucky half-back, first played for Salford at Oldham in 1902, deputising for the indisposed Ben Griffiths. After taking part in twelve of the next thirteen matches, he made way for Griffiths' return to the side in March, thereby missing a possible appearance for Salford in the 1903 Challenge Cup final. The following season, he missed just one match as Salford raced to joint top of the championship table, playing his part in the unsuccessful decider with Bradford at Halifax.

In January 1905, Dai John arrived at The Willows and the pair soon struck a firm understanding at half-back as they became one of the most respected combinations in the Northern Union. Inspired by the wily duo, Salford were back in the Challenge Cup final in 1906 and Preston's fate rested on overcoming Bradford once more, this time at Headingley. Again, Preston was to settle for being runner-up as the Yorkshire side repeated the 5-0 scoreline of two years previously. That was to be his last fling for a winner's medal. Although Salford reached the Challenge Cup semi-finals of 1907 and 1910 and the championship semi-final in 1910,

they failed to progress to the final.

In September 1905, he appeared in a trial match for Lancashire, winning a place in the county side that played Cumberland at Wigan the following month. He did not make any further appearances, although he did take part in another county trial in September 1909, but that did not mature into further selection. He did play, however, for Salford against the first touring teams to visit these shores, from New Zealand in 1907 and Australia the following year. After losing 9-2 to the Kiwis he contributed a goal to the 9-9 draw with the Aussies.

Catastrophe struck Preston on 7 January 1911 at Wigan when a seemingly innocuous dislocated shoulder brought a sudden end to his glittering career. The injury would not heal and it was almost three years later in a match at Barrow on 15 November 1913 that he came back, but broke down, never to play again. On 15 July 1916, the *Sporting Chronicle* announced that, tragically, he was killed in action during the First World War in France.

Dai Rees

Forward, 1904-1912

Birthplace: Dinas
Signed from: Llwynpia RU

Debut: 5 November 1904 v. Hull Kingston Rovers (home)
Final match: 13 January 1912 v. Wigan (home)

Appearances: 198
Tries: 14
Goals: 0
Points: 42

Representative honours: Wales, Other Nationalities, Lancashire, Glamorgan RU
Club honours: none

David (Dai) Rees was one of several players that Salford plundered from the Llwynpia Rugby Union club during their early days in the Northern Union. Aged twenty-three, the Glamorgan county player signed for the Reds on 16 August 1904. After losing five of the opening nine matches of that season, Salford gave him his debut in November against Hull Kingston Rovers. He managed to steady the ship, missing just two matches over the remainder of the season as he helped Salford to finish a respectable sixth in the table.

In the following campaign, the Reds finished well down in eighteenth position, but it was a different story in the Challenge Cup. Salford had built up a good cup reputation, reaching the semi-final or final most seasons during the period, much of it achieved on the back of their fearsome pack, of which the rampaging Rees became a prominent member. At the climax to that 1905/06 campaign, they reached their fourth Challenge Cup final in seven seasons, although for Rees it would be the only one of his career. Despite the best efforts of Rees and his colleagues, they lost a tightly contested final 5-0 to Bradford at Headingley. Rees played in two further semi-finals in 1907 and 1910 against Oldham and

Hull respectively but was in the losing side on both occasions.

Five months after signing for Salford, Rees appeared in his first international, representing the Other Nationalities against England on 2 January 1905 at Park Avenue, Bradford. The following January – on New Year's Day – he played for them again at Wigan, also against England. The Other Nationalities was largely composed of Welsh players but it was not until New Year's Day 1908 that Wales finally took to the field autonomously. On that day, Rees was the only Salford player in the side for their first match at Aberdare against the New Zealand tourists. A crowd of 15,000 saw Wales get off to a winning start 9-8. Later in the year, on 28 December, Wales played England at Broughton, with Rees again the lone 'Salfordian' in a side heavily beaten 31-7. Playing for Salford also qualified Rees to represent Lancashire and he made his first appearance for the county in October 1905 against Cumberland at Wigan, playing in seven matches over the next four years.

In August 1909, he was joined at Salford by his brother, Charlie.

Birthplace: Aberaman, near Aberdare
Signed from: Penygraig RU

Debut: 4 September 1897 v. St Helens (home)
Final match: 6 October 1906 v. Warrington (away)

Appearances: 286
Tries: 3
Goals: 1
Points: 11

Representative honours: Other Nationalities, Lancashire, Wales RU, Glamorgan RU
Club honours: none

John, alias 'Johnny' or 'Jack', Rhapps – some Welsh sources give the spelling as 'Rapps' – joined Salford for £40 at the commencement of 1897/98, their second season in the Northern Union. He arrived with a fearsome reputation as a hard-hitting forward, which he demonstrated amply in his days with Salford, earning the name 'The Salford Lion'. He had represented Wales against England at Newport in January 1897 aged twenty and was the first Welsh Rugby Union international to go north after the 1895 split with the RFU.

He was one of the most respected members of a Salford pack feared throughout the sport, particularly when it came to the Northern Union (later Rugby League) Challenge Cup. In his first two seasons at Salford, they reached the semi-final each time but the second, against Hunslet in April 1899, became notorious. Salford had five players – all forwards – dismissed, including Rhapps, who was the first to go just before the interval for a late tackle on the legendary Albert Goldthorpe. Along with three colleagues he was suspended until the following January. On returning, it was third time unlucky for Rhapps, Salford reaching the 1900 final only to lose 16-8 to Swinton and he subsequently appeared in three more losing finals for Salford in 1902, 1903 and 1906. A further disappointment was in 1904, being in the team beaten in a championship play-off with Bradford.

Invited to a Lancashire county trial in October 1898 at Warrington, he failed to convince the selectors, but two years later at St Helens in a further trial match he managed to do so, making his debut against Cumberland in Workington during October 1900. It was the first of 14 appearances by the Welshman for his adopted county. His career ended before Wales played their first match but he did represent the Other Nationalities – in the first ever Northern Union (Rugby League) international – against England at Wigan in April 1904.

In the absence of Jimmy Lomas – representing Cumberland – he captained the Salford team at Warrington on 6 October 1906. He missed the next match, a report claiming he was 'having a rest'. It was to be a long one, as he did not play again, the club officially announcing his retirement in August 1907. He later became groundsman at Ardwick Athletic ground until it closed down in the 1920s.

Maurice Richards

Wing three-quarter, 1969-1983

Birthplace: Ystrad Rhondda
Signed from: Cardiff RU

Debut: 15 October 1969 v. Leigh (home)
Final match: 21 August 1983 v. Wigan (home)

Appearances: 498 (includes 2 as substitute)
Tries: 297
Goals: 32
Points: 956

Representative honours: Tourist 1974, Great Britain, Wales, British Lions RU, Wales RU
Club honours: Rugby League Championship 1973/74 and 1975/76, Lancashire Cup 1972, BBC2 Floodlit Cup 1974/75

Maurice Charles Rees Richards is the proud holder of two major records at Salford: the most official games ever played with 498 appearances and the most tries scored, at 297. Both records fell, predictably towards the end of his career, in 1982. His achievement was recognised by the directors through the award of an inscribed carriage clock. The capture of Richards, a left wing three-quarter, was a major coup from Welsh Rugby Union circles in October 1969, signing for a reported £7,000 fee from the Cardiff Rugby Union Club.

The former British Lion had won immediate fame when he scored four tries for Wales against England at Cardiff Arms Park the previous April, equalling the long-standing records of Willie Llewellyn (1899) and Reggie Gibbs (1908). Apart from playing for his beloved Wales nine times he also went on the British Lions tour in 1968 to South Africa, playing in the First, Third (alongside future Salford colleague Mike Coulman) and Fourth Tests. He also toured Australasia and Fiji with Wales in 1969.

Initially he had played both soccer and rugby at school: 'My family often took me to watch soccer at Cardiff City, but there was no

chance of me taking it up seriously – I simply was not good enough', explained Richards. Playing Rugby Union for his school as a centre, he was picked for the Welsh schoolboys team and was quickly snapped up by Cardiff Rugby Union club: 'Playing for Cardiff straight from school was one of the great moments in my rugby career – a schoolboy's dream'. With an abundance of centres already at the club, he went on the wing – a position he would fill throughout his career.

In 1969, a strange event happened in Richards' life that was to shape the remainder of his rugby career. Talking with friends at work about rugby, the conversation went on to Rugby League and Richards commented that it would be an interesting challenge. Unknown to him, his friend contacted Salford saying Richards could be interested in switching codes. 'It was as simple as that. Salford got in touch with me and I finally signed for the club in chairman Brian Snape's home at Wilmslow in the early hours of one morning.' The date was 15 October 1969 and, later that same day, he made his debut against Leigh at The Willows. Being pushed into his first match so quickly did not faze him, his pre-match comment being: 'I'm not worried. I will be happy to play and get the feel of the game and I will be happy to get it over. I expect to be played on, I would be surprised if I wasn't'. In his match report in the *Manchester Evening News*, Jack McNamara said: 'He is alert, has anticipation, and good hands. All things considered, Richards need have no worries about his chances of succeeding.'

Richards became a great favourite at Salford, where his changes of pace and deceptive running thrilled the crowds. He made his first appearance for Wales only eight days after signing for Salford, playing at The Willows against France. Richards played in the centre for once, with his former Cardiff team-mate Frank Wilson on the wing. During his long career in Rugby League, Richards appeared to shy away from international matches. He played only twice more for Wales and turned down the opportunity to join the Welsh World Cup squad for Australia and New Zealand in 1975. Similarly, with Great Britain he was to play, amazingly considering his talent, in only two Test matches. These were both on the 1974 tour Down Under, when he flew out as a replacement. His one other representative selection was as a substitute for the Other Nationalities side, at county level, against Lancashire at The Willows in 1974, but, in the event he did not leave the bench.

With Salford, he led the club try charts five times, twice setting post-war records (later broken by Keith Fielding) and he was Rugby League's top try scorer in 1975/76 with 37. He scored tries in eight consecutive matches from August to September 1975 (bettered only by Bob Brown's nine in 1934 at the time) and played in 97 consecutive matches for the Reds from August 1971 to September 1973. He was a member of Salford's two championship squads of the 1970s and in the victorious teams that took the Lancashire Cup in 1972 and the Floodlit Cup in 1974/75. He also played in the beaten final teams for the Players Trophy in 1973, Premiership in 1976, and Lancashire Cup in 1974 and 1975 – he missed the 1973 final due to a damaged cartilage. Richards later said: 'My greatest

Maurice Richards – heading for the try line once again!

moment with Salford was probably winning the Lancashire Cup in 1972, because it was the first thing I won with Salford'. Richards received a deserved testimonial in 1980, which raised £9,700.

After playing in a pre-season friendly with Dewsbury the previous week, he was in the team for the first league match of the 1983/84 season against Wigan at the Willows. The Reds lost 14-16 and Richards registered his final try – Salford's first under the new 'four-point' rule – before unexpectedly retiring. A combination of a groin injury and work commitments was the apparent reason, but he eventually returned to training in November 1983, after Coulman had taken over as coach from Malcolm Aspey, and played in a reserve team match in January 1984, but drifted away from the club after that.

Robert Gate perfectly summed up the unassuming Richards in his book *Gone North – Volume 2* (1988): 'Although Richards scored many, many spectacular tries from deep positions he was never a flamboyant character, always appearing cool and unaffected. He simply got on with the job of scoring tries. His conduct was never less than exemplary.'

A.J.F. (Gus) Risman

Full-back/centre three-quarter/stand-off half, 1929-1946

Birthplace: Cardiff
Signed from: Cardiff Scottish RU

Debut: 31 August 1929 v. Barrow (home)
Final match: 23 March 1946 v. Rochdale Hornets (home)

Appearances: 427
Tries: 143
Goals: 796
Points: 2021

Representative honours: Tourist 1932, 1936 and 1946 (tour captain), Great Britain, Wales, England, Glamorgan & Monmouthshire
Club honours: Rugby League Championship 1932/33, 1936/37, 1938/39, 1940/41 (Bradford Northern), 1941/42 (Dewsbury) and 1950/51 (Workington Town), Rugby League Challenge Cup 1938, 1942 (Leeds) and 1952 (Workington Town), Lancashire Cup 1931, 1934, 1935 and 1936, Yorkshire Cup 1941 (Bradford Northern), Lancashire League Championship 1932/33, 1933/34, 1934/35, 1936/37 and 1938/39

Augustus John Ferdinand ('Gus') Risman is considered by many knowledgeable critics to be the greatest player ever to wear the red jersey of Salford, a view endorsed by the fact that he was one of the original eight inductees into the Rugby League Hall of Fame in October 1988. Signed by the Reds in 1929, when he was seventeen, he became the complete all-rounder – the supreme master tactician, an inspiring captain and, in later years, a successful coach. He appeared in his last match for Salford in 1946, but continued as a player until 1954, possibly the longest span ever in professional Rugby League.

Moving from his birthplace, Cardiff, to Barry at an early age, he first played rugby at the Barry County School and joined the Dinas Powis club. He was invited to play for Cardiff Scottish and, at his first match in Stroud, was approached by a Rugby League scout, Frank Young. Young offered to set up a trial with his former club, Leeds, who declined, but Young arranged one with Salford instead. At the end of the 1928/29 season, he played in Salford's reserves and impressed sufficiently to be signed during the summer. Alf Beecroft, of the *Salford City Reporter*,

remembered: 'A mere seventeen-year-old, he was recruited as being full of promise. Not immediately impressive, he came on by leaps and bounds, equally at home at full-back or centre. A great stylist, strong and tricky runner and a fine goal-kicker, he soon made his presence felt and revolutionised the team's back play.'

With Salford, whom he captained from 1936 until his departure in 1946, Risman was to win everything on offer. After three months, he found himself at full-back in his first big match – the 1929 Lancashire Cup final. On that occasion, Salford lost 15-2 to Warrington, but Salford – and Risman – played in five more county finals over the next nine seasons, winning four. The Rugby League Championship was re-captured, after a nineteen-year gap, in 1933. This feat was repeated twice more during the decade, although they lost the 1934 decider. In the championship final of 1937 – his benefit year – with the score at 11-11, Risman coolly kicked his fifth goal in the final minutes to win the trophy by the narrowest of margins over Warrington. The biggest, and most elusive, prize was the Wembley showpiece Challenge Cup final, a dream ultimately fulfilled in 1938 with the victory over Barrow, although a speedy return in 1939 was to end in disappointment.

Risman achieved several landmarks at Salford. He broke the club goalscoring record twice and became the first player at the club to top 100 goals in a season. His 116 in 1933/34 stood until David Watkins beat it in 1970/71. Similarly, Risman's record of 277 points that same season remained until Watkins arrived on the scene. Risman was Salford's leading goal and point scorer for eight consecutive seasons. In 1938/39, he was the top scorer in the Rugby League with 267 points. He set a club record for goals in a match, scoring thirteen against Bramley (1933) and Broughton Rangers (1940). During the war years, he guested for several clubs, winning the championship in 1941 with Bradford Northern and in 1942 with Dewsbury. He added the Yorkshire Cup to his collection with Bradford in 1941 and another Challenge Cup success in 1942, playing for Leeds.

Risman has many representative honours in Rugby League. The biggest of all was playing for Great Britain on tour, something he achieved three times, in 1932, 1936 and 1946. Although not the tour captain in 1936, he led the team in the Third Test against Australia and both Tests in New Zealand. His ultimate honour was captaining that first post-war tour in 1946, the so-called 'Indomitables', named after the aircraft carrier that transported them. 'Travelling on a carrier gave us wonderful facilities for training' said Risman in an *Open Rugby* interview in 1983. 'We were able to use the huge flight decks, which were some 150 yards long. That meant we could sprint, practice moves and do just about every type of training possible on shore. By the time we arrived in Freemantle we were easily the fittest Rugby League team that had ever landed in Australia.' His first Test match was on the 1932 tour – the third of the rubber – against Australia in Sydney.

Altogether, Risman represented Britain seventeen times, including five Test series against the Aussies. He was picked for Wales on eighteen occasions, playing his part in three European Championship wins by the Principality. His debut in the Welsh jersey, in March 1931 against England at Huddersfield, was his first representative Rugby League

Gus Risman, in full flight, prepares to side-step past a would-be tackler.

match of any description. He also, surprisingly, represented England in Paris during 1934, in the first international played by France. His other, numerous, selections include the Northern Rugby League (against Australia in 1933), the British Empire XIII (versus France in 1937) and the English RL (taking on the French RL in 1946). He played county Rugby League for Glamorgan and Monmouthshire on three occasions in 1931/32.

Returning from the 1946 tour, he signed for the fledgling Workington Town as player-coach and took them to both championship and Wembley success in six seasons, perhaps his greatest achievement. He made 301 appearances for Town before leaving in 1954, following a dispute over signing players. He played nine times for Batley at the end of 1954 before retiring as a player. He was manager at Salford from 1956 to 1960, but could not repeat the success he enjoyed in Cumberland and later managed Oldham and Bradford Northern. Fifty years after becoming an original Red Devil during Salford's historic tour of France, he returned as a guest of the club when they met Catalan in 1984.

Jack Roberts

Forward/three-quarter, 1883-1895

Birthplace: Bolton
Signed from: Egerton

Debut: 3 March 1883 v. Broughton Rangers (away)
Final match: 16 March 1895 v. St Helens (home)

Appearances: 271
Tries: 100
Goals: 1

Representative honours: Lancashire RU
Club honours: Lancashire RU Club Championship 1892/93

John William Roberts – otherwise known as 'Jack' – joined Salford in 1882, playing mostly in the reserves for the 1882/83 season where, having a reputation as a sprinter, he scored thirteen tries. At the end of the term he was given two outings in the first team, playing in the three-quarter line at Broughton Rangers in March, scoring his side's only try to earn a draw. A month later he appeared amongst the forwards against Bolton at the Reds' New Barnes enclosure. In his second season, lining up mostly in the three-quarters, he scored 17 tries in only 19 matches, easily breaking Hugh Williamson's club record two years earlier of 10. He led the list again in 1884/85 (14 tries) and 1888/89 (10).

In 1889/90 on 15 February, he scored five tries in Salford's seventeen-try blitz against Manchester Free Wanderers; both are record figures for the club under the RFU label. He was actually playing in the pack that day and completed the season with 18 touchdowns, just four less than the club's flying wingman, Frank Miles. Roberts' final figures for Salford of 271 appearances and 100 tries, place him second in both those categories during the club's Rugby Union era.

He moved from the three-quarters into the forwards in 1886 with great success and started to gain the attention of the county selectors. On 12 March 1887, he made his first appearance for Lancashire, playing in the high-profile match against Middlesex at The Oval in celebration of Queen Victoria's Jubilee. Later that year, in November, he was in the team that met Cheshire at Aigburth, near Liverpool. He was chosen for a further two matches in February 1889 – against Somerset and Cumberland – before making his fifth, and final, appearance for the county on 9 March 1891, opposing Ulster at Whalley Range.

His proudest moments with Salford were playing as vice-captain against the Maori touring side in March 1889 and being in the team that won the 1892/93 Lancashire Club Championship. The following season, however, he did not play for the club at all, reports stating that 'Roberts was "shaky" about turning up'. He did return for the 1894/95 campaign, where he played another eleven times before retiring after a career that had spanned thirteen seasons, the longest by any Salford player under Rugby Union rules.

Steve Rule

Stand-off half/full-back, 1978-1983

Birthplace: Bebington, Merseyside
Signed from: Sale RU

Debut: 24 February 1978 v. Bramley (home)
Final match: 24 April 1983 v. Dewsbury (away)

Appearances: 123 (includes 6 as substitute)
Tries: 23
Goals: 395
Points: 848

Representative honours: Wales, Cheshire RU
Club honours: none

Steve Rule was described by one journalist as a 'point scoring machine' and that certainly appeared to be the case as he kicked goals for Salford with uncanny ease and accuracy. After landing seven goals at Warrington, even Widnes referee Ronnie Campbell praised his kicking: 'I've never seen a kicker like him. I can't figure out how he does it. I stood behind him, and the ball swirled through the air in a wavy line and the touch judges said it was hard to follow. They were unsure until the last second that a goal had been scored'. Salford had signed Rule from near-neighbours Sale Rugby Union club for £2,000 in February 1978. Before joining Sale, he had played for Birkenhead Park and Loughborough Colleges, had trials for England and represented the English Universities and Cheshire county.

After an outstanding reserve team debut, he made his first senior appearance in the centre against Bramley in a 9-7 Challenge Cup win. With some uncertainty as to his best placing, he was tried at stand off – his Rugby Union position – the next season taking up the goal-kicking duties when David Watkins was unavailable. With the departure of Watkins, he settled in at the vacated full-back slot in 1979/80 and took on the goal-kicking responsibilities full time, registering 134 during the season. Following an injury hit year – due to a badly torn groin – he landed another 130 in 1981/82. In September 1981, he equalled the club record when he kicked 13 goals from 13 attempts against Doncaster. Although he eventually settled in well at Salford, he confessed in an interview with Jack McNamara: 'I had difficulty in adapting to League. The problem was positional and I did not get much help from the coach, Stan McCormick. Even from the kick-off, I did not know where to stand. Although it sounds simple, it is difficult for a newcomer. In League you try to force the opposition inside while in Union you try to get them going wide'. Rule credited his ex-Sale team-mate, Gordon Graham with helping him settle.

On 18 March 1981, Rule played his only international match for Wales – courtesy of a Welsh grandfather – in the clash with England at Craven Park, Hull. He joined St Helens in the summer of 1983 in exchange for Peter Glynn.

Joe Shaw

Forward, 1884-1891

Birthplace: Manchester
Signed from: unknown

Debut: 12 April 1884 v. Cheetham (home)
Final match: 7 November 1891 v. Liverpool (away)

Appearances: 195
Tries: 16
Goals: 24

Representative honours: none
Club honours: none

Joseph Edwin Shaw made his Salford debut in the final match of the 1883/84 season in the victory over Cheetham on 12 April. Born on 27 April 1863 in Manchester, he was two weeks short of his twenty-first birthday. Known to be living in Pendleton at the time, it is uncertain which club he played for before Salford.

By the 1885/86 season he was commanding a regular place in the forwards and, in fact, the only match for Salford when he did not appear with the pack was against Manchester Rangers at New Barnes on 10 April 1886. On that occasion, he was at full-back and finished as the hero of the afternoon. His drop goal – the only one he scored for Salford – saved the day, as they appeared to be heading for a shock defeat. One match report exclaimed: 'Shaw's was a most creditable performance and the spectators testified their joy in as lusty a cheer as I have ever heard at New Barnes. To him belonged the honour of making this game a draw in favour of the home team.' The game finished level at one goal each, the reference that it was 'in favour' of Salford was due to the scoring of six 'minor' points (when the defence is forced to touch down behind its own line) to their visitors' one. Although not contributing to the score, it indicated moral victory.

Shaw replaced the departed Jack Anderton as the club's place kicker in 1888/89, scoring 12 and finishing the season as leading goalscorer. He registered a further 10 the following season, sharing top spot with half-back Sam Walch. His biggest day with Salford came in the March 1889 meeting against the touring Maori side at New Barnes. Later that year, in October, he was included in the Lancashire county trial match at Whalley Range. Unfortunately, he could not press his claim further in the selectors' eyes and, in fact, never did appear for the county.

Having lost his regular first team place in 1890/91 he transferred to Broughton Rangers, his introduction for them being against St Helens Recs on 21 November 1891, two weeks after his final Salford outing. He played regularly with the Rangers until the mid-1890s. The final match of his career was when he represented them at Hull on 23 November 1895 – the first Northern Union season – signing off with a try, their only score in an 8-3 defeat.

Peter Smethurst

Prop forward/second row forward, 1967-1970

Birthplace: Swinton
Signed from: Oldham

Debut: 8 September 1967 v. Halifax (away)
Final match: 26 December 1970 v. Barrow (home)

Appearances: 124 (includes 3 as substitute)
Tries: 10
Goals: 1
Points: 32

Representative honours: none
Club honours: Rugby League Challenge Cup 1971 (Leigh), Lancashire Cup 1973 (Wigan), Second Division Championship 1963/64 (Oldham), Lancashire League Championship 1960/61 (Swinton)

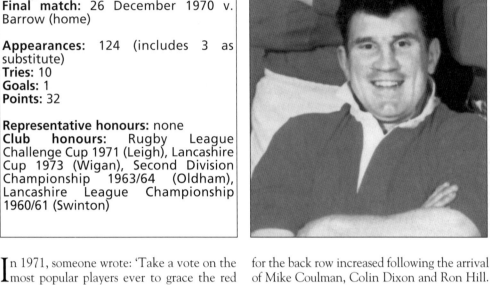

In 1971, someone wrote: 'Take a vote on the most popular players ever to grace the red shirt of Salford and one man will stand out because he will be on everyone's list. That man is Peter Smethurst. His joy in the game is seen in every match he plays, and in every match he plays wholeheartedly, keeping nothing back, running, tackling, covering, pushing, sweating, revelling, encouraging – but mostly laughing.' These words appeared in a Salford programme a year after he had left the club and conveyed the affection felt for Smethurst at The Willows.

He had joined Swinton from the local Swinton Methodists side in 1955 where, playing as a centre three-quarter, he gained the attention of Oldham, who paid £3,500 for him in September 1961. It was at Oldham, playing more often in the second row, where he started to grab the headlines. On 8 September 1967, Salford moved in with a £3,250 fee, Smethurst making his debut at Halifax the same day.

Over the next three years, Smethurst won the hearts of the Salford fans, giving the proverbial 110 per cent every time he appeared. He temporarily lost his place midway through the 1968/69 season, when competition

for the back row increased following the arrival of Mike Coulman, Colin Dixon and Ron Hill. It cost him an appearance in the 1969 Wembley final, frustratingly sitting it out on the substitutes' bench.

He returned to favour the following season and was a regular choice until his shock transfer to Leigh in December 1970. Salford had signed Bill Kirkbride from Castleford and, suddenly, he was surplus to requirements. A disappointed Smethurst vowed: 'I was very happy at The Willows. I will do everything to show that the small fee Salford are getting for me is as good as the thousands they have lashed out.' Smethurst was true to his word, first as a Wembley winner with Leigh in 1971, and then capturing a Lancashire Cup winner's medal with Wigan in 1973, ironically against favourites Salford. For Smethurst, it was third time lucky, having lost in the Lancashire finals of 1960 (with Swinton) and 1966 (with Oldham).

After he finished playing in 1977, Smethurst rejoined Salford as reserve team coach but it was short-lived. Two months later, he was back at Wigan on their coaching staff, followed by similar appointments at Leigh (1982/83) and Oldham (1983/84).

Dan Smith
Full-back, 1897-1904

Birthplace: Swansea
Signed from: Swansea RU

Debut: 4 September 1897 v. St Helens (home)
Final match: 28 April 1904 v. Bradford (at Halifax)

Appearances: 218
Tries: 1
Goals: 14
Points: 31

Representative honours: Other Nationalities, Lancashire
Club honours: none

To Daniel Smith fell the unenviable task of taking over at full-back from the great Billy Manwaring, who had retired at the end of the previous season, having defended the citadel with valour for eleven campaigns. Salford had searched carefully to find a replacement and the Welshman appeared to fit the bill perfectly. He had played much of his rugby in the three-quarters with Swansea RUFC due to the presence of the famous Welsh full-back William Bancroft, who earned 33 caps for Wales. One report, announcing the capture, said: 'Smith, of Swansea, one of the best players in Wales, will succeed Manwaring. At Swansea, he was a splendid understudy for Bancroft and did well for the Welshmen. At three-quarter Smith is noted for his fast play and has rendered excellent service to his former colleagues.'

Smith made his first appearance on the opening day of the 1897/98 season and quickly settled in, missing only one match towards the end of the term. He built a reputation for being one of the best kickers of the ball from hand that Salford ever had. During his seven seasons with the Reds, he was virtually an ever-present, missing only 18 matches and in 1900/01 never missed a game.

He played in three Challenge Cup finals for Salford in 1900, 1902 and 1903 but all ended in defeat. In 1904, he was also involved in the championship decider, which went the way of Bradford – this was his final appearance for Salford.

The frustration of missing club honours was relieved somewhat by his personal achievements at county and international level. On 3 October 1900, he joined the ranks of Lancashire's adopted sons from the Valleys when included in the county trial match St Helens. He had an excellent match and, seventeen days later, he made his county bow at Workington's Lonsdale Park against Cumberland. He kept his place and was in the team against Yorkshire and Cheshire during the same season. He played 12 times for Lancashire, the last being at Wigan on 13 January 1904, with Cumberland as the opposition. Although his county career had run its course, he was involved in the first international match. Staged at Wigan on 5 April 1904, an all-Welsh side, including Smith, curiously posed as the Other Nationalities for the match against England. Shortly afterwards he retired and moved to Canada.

Fergie Southward

Centre three-quarter/wing three-quarter, 1921-1933

Birthplace: Dearham, near Maryport
Signed from: Brookland Rovers RU

Debut: 22 January 1921 v. Barrow (home)
Final match: 8 April 1933 v. St Helens Recs (home)

Appearances: 340
Tries: 90
Goals: 158
Points: 586

Representative honours: Cumberland
Club honours: Lancashire Cup 1931, Lancashire League Championship 1932/33

Ferguson Southward – forever remembered as 'Fergie' – was born in 1900 at Dearham on the Cumbrian coast. He began at Dearham Rugby Union club before moving on to Brookland Rovers, joining Salford in 1921. He is probably the club's most famous player from the era of the 1920s, playing most of his career in the centre, moving to the wing in the latter years.

Although only slightly built, he had strong shoulders and was a tough competitor, possessing an excellent sidestep. He led Salford's point chart for five consecutive seasons, was the leading try scorer in three and top goalscorer in four. He stayed loyal to Salford during one of the low periods of the club's history, when the match with the New Zealanders in November 1926, although lost 10-18, was the only high point.

Things changed when Lance Todd arrived in 1928 and, as captain for a while, he found himself in a side that was looking down the table instead of up it! He was not in the side for the 1929 Lancashire Cup final but was in the 1931 team to meet Swinton at The Cliff ground in Broughton. Playing on the wing, Southward kicked two goals in the 10-8 victory. The match report said: 'The man who drove the nail in Swinton's coffin was Southward, for ten years connected with the Weaste club and who this season has come back with a vengeance'. In his final season of 1932/33, he earned a Lancashire League Championship medal, playing in nine of the matches.

Although he waited patiently for success at club level, he had a very distinguished career for his county, Cumberland. He was selected for the first time against Yorkshire in October 1922 at Maryport, playing centre in a 9-4 defeat. A month later, demonstrating his versatility, he played stand-off half in the meeting with Lancashire at Swinton's former Chorley Road ground. He kicked three goals but was on the wrong side of a 46-9 hammering. He became a regular fixture in the county team and played every year until his final match – his twenty-sixth – in October 1932 against Lancashire at Barrow when the 9-3 victory gave Cumberland the county title. He also celebrated county championship success in 1927. In 1945, he became the first coach of Workington Town.

Evan Thomas
Forward, 1905-1916

Birthplace: Pillgwinlly, Newport
Signed from: Pillgwinlly Harriers RU

Debut: 2 September 1905 v. Hull (home)
Final match: 8 January 1916 (wartime match) v. Leigh (home)

Appearances: 311 (includes 4in wartime)
Tries: 24
Goals: 0
Points: 72

Representative honours: Wales
Club honours: Rugby League Championship 1913/14

Evan J. Thomas, at over 6 ft 2 in and 13 stone, was considered to be a Welsh forward giant for the period in which he played for Salford. He arrived at The Willows, aged twenty-three, in August 1905, having had second thoughts about joining the police force and travelled north instead. At the end of his first term, he was playing in a Challenge Cup final, Bradford providing the opposition at Headingley. Although Salford lost 5-0, Thomas must have felt after just one season in the game, that success was 'around the corner'. Any optimism that he may have carried into the next season was misplaced, however, for despite Salford having appeared in four of the last seven finals, it would be thirty-two years before the next. Thomas did at least reach the semi-final stage with Salford in 1907 and 1910.

It was in the championship that he would find his ultimate reward. Even so, when Salford reached the top four play-off for the first time in 1909/10, receiving a home semi-final with Wigan – the reward for finishing second in the table – they fluffed their chance, losing 17-6. Four years later, they were in an identical position, finishing second in the league and facing Wigan at The Willows. Much to the relief of Thomas and Salford they did not fail a second time, going through 16-5. The final against Huddersfield gave Thomas his greatest moment in Rugby League, as the mighty Fartowners were defeated 5-3, on a day when Thomas and the rest of Salford's pack stood firm, putting in a resolute tackling stint to deny the Yorkshiremen in the second half.

Thomas played on two occasions for Wales, both ending in defeats by England, the first being at Ebbw Vale on 1 April 1910, and the second at St Helens on 14 February 1914. Lancashire invited him to their trial match in September 1906 and again in September 1907, but he did not win his place in the county side on either occasion. The First World War effectively ended his career and he played his last competitive match for Salford on 5 April 1915 at Oldham, when he scored his 24th and final try for the Reds in a 19-8 defeat. During the season of 1915/16, he managed to appear in four of the wartime friendly games before finally hanging up his boots.

Harold Thomas

Second row forward, 1937-1945

Birthplace: Neath
Signed from: Neath RU

Debut: 9 October 1937 v. St Helens Recs (home)
Final match: 22 December 1945 v. Broughton Rangers (away)

Appearances: 119
Tries: 6
Goals: 0
Points: 18

Representative honours: Wales, Wales RU
Club honours: Rugby League Championship 1938/39, Rugby League Challenge Cup 1938, Lancashire League Championship 1938/39

The Salford career of Harold Watkin Thomas was disappointingly short, courtesy of the Second World War, but he packed some of the club's greatest moments into his 119 appearances after Salford obtained his services for £375 in September 1937.

A strong running back row, he was considered one of the most outstanding forwards in Welsh Rugby Union. He became team captain at Neath in 1936/37 at twenty-two, and was in the Neath-Aberavon XV against the 1935 All Blacks. He won six caps for Wales, the first against England at Swansea in January 1936, Wales winning the international championship that year.

His debut for Salford was at prop, a position he occupied in his first nine matches, until Todd swapped him around with Dai Davies – another recent acquisition from the Valleys – for a match with Liverpool Stanley in January 1938. The move cemented a solid back-row with Paddy Dalton and Jack Feetham, a combination that graced Wembley at the end of the season. It was Thomas' first big day in Rugby League and he was not to be disappointed, as Salford beat Barrow 7-4.

In many respects, 1938/39 was even better for the Welsh second-rower. He began with the Lancashire Cup final in October against Wigan, which the men from Central Park won 10-7. A few weeks later, he was in the Wales team to oppose England at Llanelli, a match that produced a 17-9 win for the host country. In April, he travelled to Bordeaux to play against France but, this time, Wales went down 16-10. Sadly, it was to be his last Rugby League appearance for Wales. His whirlwind season moved on and, the following month, he was back at Wembley in another Challenge Cup final. This time the result went the wrong way for Thomas as Halifax won the last pre-war final 20-3. A week later and he was in his only championship final at Maine Road, Manchester. In front of a massive 69,504 crowd, he shared in an 8-6 victory over Castleford. A further medal came his way as the 1938/39 season saw Salford crowned Lancashire League Championship winners for the fifth time in the decade.

In the first post-war season of 1945/46, he played just 9 matches before retiring. He returned to Wales and, for a while, managed the Neath team in the Welsh Rugby League.

111

Willie Thomas

Centre three-quarter, 1903-1921

Birthplace: Swansea
Signed from: Aberavon RU

Debut: 5 September 1903 v. Batley (away)
Final match: 31 December 1921 v. Widnes (home)

Appearances: 501 (includes 57 in wartime)
Tries: 99 (includes 7 in wartime)
Goals: 68 (includes 6 in wartime)
Points: 433 (includes 33 in wartime)

Representative honours: Wales, Other Nationalities
Club honours: Rugby League Championship 1913/14

Welsh right-centre William S. (Willie) Thomas signed for Salford in August 1903 from the Aberavon Rugby Union club. He is the only player to make 500 appearances for the Reds, taking into account his contribution during the period of the First World War.

Taking over the team captaincy, following the departure of Jimmy Lomas in 1911, the highpoint of his career was the day he masterminded Salford's unexpected victory over the mighty Huddersfield 'Team of All Talents' in the 1914 Championship final. Salford had gained a slight advantage in that their semi-final tie had taken place on the previous Saturday when, inspired by two tries from Thomas, they eliminated Wigan 16-5. Huddersfield's play-off match, against Hull, was not played until Monday and, as expected, Huddersfield won convincingly. The delay allowed Thomas the luxury of travelling over to Fartown to watch the match on a spying mission, upon which he planned his team's defensive strategy.

In the final, Salford had to fight their way back after the Yorkshire side had taken an early 3-0 start, but a converted try in the corner gave the Reds the slenderest of interval leads. In the second half, Salford resisted terrific pressure, putting in some tremendous and inspired tackling, with Thomas leading the way, containing the threat of their famous centre, Harold Wagstaff. There was no further scoring and Salford held on to win 5-3. Delighted captain Thomas was carried shoulder-high from the field at the finish. When they arrived in Salford with the trophy he said: 'If we felt proud at the moment of victory when we knew we had beaten the great Huddersfield side, we felt prouder still when we got back to Salford and found such a welcome awaiting us'. For Salford, it was an historic day, being the first trophy won since leaving the RFU in 1896.

Thomas made an impressive debut with Salford in September 1903, scoring two tries in a 13-3 win at Batley. Not only was he to prove himself as a sound defender but, at 5 ft 9 in and 12 stone, he was an elegant, elusive centre and a fine distributor of the ball. In 1904, he appeared in his first big game for Salford. It was a championship decider against Bradford at Halifax, the two clubs having finished level at the top of the table. Bradford capitalised on a mistake-ridden Salford performance to win 5-0 through a late try.

Two years later, Thomas was again up against Bradford on a high-profile occasion. This time, it was to settle the destination of the

Proud captain Willie Thomas with his team in 1913/14, destined to become Salford's first championship season. From left to right, back row: Harry Goldsmith, George Thom, Bob Ritchie, Jack Bevon, Charlie Rees, George Currie. Middle row: George Callender, Bernard Mesley, Thomas, Arthur Loveluck, Joe White (trainer). Front row: Harry Launce, Dai John, Edgar May.

1906 Challenge Cup. Played at Headingley, a late try again gave Bradford a 5-0 victory.

Despite his excellence, Thomas gained surprisingly few representative honours. He scored a try for the Other Nationalities against England in April 1904 at Wigan in the first ever Rugby League international but waited seven years for his next chance, playing for Wales versus England at Ebbw Vale in April 1911. It was his only appearance for the Principality, although he did play for the combined Wales and West of England team in a match against the 1911 Kangaroos at Ashton Gate, Bristol, on 20 December. Earlier that month he had captained Salford against the tourists, the Aussies winning 6-3. It was the third time he had taken on a touring side with the Reds, having previously been in the line-up that lost 9-2 to the first New Zealand tourists of 1907, and playing his part in the epic 9-9 draw with the 1908 Australians.

His otherwise perfect copybook got itself tarnished in January 1915, when he was suspended by the Northern Union for five matches when he was caught up in the team's refusal to make concessions in their wages for the 'Relief Fund'. After that hiccup, Thomas turned out for Salford on a regular basis through the duration of the First World War and played a further four seasons after peace resumed.

At the onset of his final campaign (1921/22), it was announced that he would retire after leading the Reds against the 1921 Australian tourists in their fourth match of the season on 17 September. To mark the occasion, he had lunch with the visitors before the game, which the Aussies won 48-3, Thomas' final try for the club being their only score. In a further function after the match, he was presented with the match ball, autographed by the Colonial players. He duly retired, but in December returned to help the club out for three matches before finishing for good. In September 1945, he joined the board at Salford.

Pat Tunney

Forward, 1897-1905

Birthplace: County Durham
Signed from: unknown

Debut: 30 October 1897 v. Wigan (away)
Final match: 2 January 1905 v. Widnes (away)

Appearances: 222
Tries: 11
Goals: 0
Points: 33

Representative honours: England, Durham & Northumberland, Lancashire, Durham RU
Club honours: none

Salford acquired Pat Tunney, a Durham County Rugby Union player in October 1897, as part of the process of building up their forward strength for the rigours of the Northern Union. In his first three seasons with Salford, the team, led by their marauding pack, reached the Challenge Cup semi-final each time. He was dismissed from the field during the first of those, making it into the final at the third attempt in 1900. The opposition in the final was Swinton, and Tunney suffered his first major disappointment in the sport as the Lions won 16-8. Two more finals soon followed, but it was to be three defeats in a row for luckless Tunney and his comrades, losing to Broughton Rangers (1902) and Halifax (1903). In April 1904, he found himself in a final of a different sort, when he was in the team that Salford took to Halifax for the championship decider with Bradford. The outcome was still the same though, with Salford emerging once more as the runners-up.

Three weeks before that championship play-off, he was chosen for the first international match staged by the Northern Union, representing England versus the Other Nationalities. Whilst Tunney was no doubt pleased to be involved in what was his only international appearance, it is amazing to realise that it was his third match in four days, having just played twice for Salford. His first recognition of any description was when asked to play in the Rest of the League team against champions Broughton Rangers in April 1899, a typical finale to the season in those days. Two years later, he again represented the Rest against the latest champions, Oldham.

In October 1899, although hailing from the North-East of England, he was offered a place in the trial match held by Lancashire at New Barnes and progressed to the county side for the fixture with Cumberland at Oldham later that same month. He played three times for the county during that season and over the next five years appeared in eighteen matches for the Lancashire side, including two against the combined Durham and Northumberland counties team. Just to make things more confused, he represented the Durham-Northumberland combination in October 1902 against Cumberland at Workington whilst continuing to turn out for Lancashire during the same season.

Silas Warwick

Forward, 1904-1911

Birthplace: Whitehaven
Signed from: Broughton Rangers

Debut: 24 December 1904 v. Leigh (home)
Final match: 9 September 1911 v. Broughton Rangers (away)

Appearances: 209
Tries: 20
Goals: 1
Points: 62

Representative honours: Great Britain, England, Cumberland
Club honours: none

Silas Warwick was the first player from Salford to play for Great Britain when he was selected for the opening Test match against the New Zealand tourists on 25 January 1908 at Headingley, appearing in the Second Test two weeks later at Stamford Bridge, London. A few months later, in April, he was in the England team for the match with Wales in Penygraig. His first representative appearance was in October 1906, wearing the Cumberland jersey in the match against Lancashire at Maryport. From then until 1910 he appeared in ten matches for his native county, including the prestige matches with the New Zealanders (January 1908 at Workington) and the Australians (February 1909, Carlisle). He also played for Salford against the New Zealand side in December 1907 but was unavailable when Salford met the Aussies in October 1908, being on duty for Cumberland at Huddersfield in the match with Yorkshire.

The signing of Warwick from borough rivals Broughton Rangers (where he had played 36 games since 1902) in November 1904 was part of a concerted effort by Salford to strengthen their squad of forwards after the disappointment of losing the previous season's championship decider. After several reserve matches, Warwick was given his chance in the Christmas Eve fixture with Leigh.

His first seasons with the club were disappointing as far as the championship was concerned, as the Reds slid down the league ladder. The competition they did continue to make inroads into – without ever taking the winner's rostrum – was the Northern Union Challenge Cup. Warwick saw action in three semi-finals, in 1906, 1907 and 1910, reaching the final in the first of those. It was the only final, of any kind, that Warwick was involved in with Salford, but it ended in personal disaster. Played at Headingley, the match against Bradford was scoreless when he was dismissed for fighting during the second half, along with Feather of Bradford. The sending off seemed to hurt Salford more than the opposition, who gratefully finished the day as 5-0 winners. Warwick continued to serve Salford until September 1911, when he suddenly departed after playing against his former club, a match in which he was reported as being 'very much to the front'. Despite that, he was 'stood down' from the team for the next fixture, not appearing in the first or reserve sides again.

David Watkins MBE

Stand-off half/centre three-quarter/full-back, 1967-1979

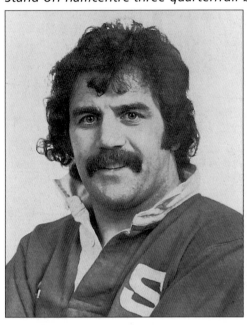

Birthplace: Blaina, Monmouthshire
Signed from: Newport RU

Debut: 20 October 1967 v. Oldham (home)
Final match: 1 April 1979 v. Rochdale Hornets (away)

Appearances: 407 (includes 2 as substitute)
Tries: 147
Goals: 1241
Points: 2907

Representative honours: Tourist 1974, Great Britain, Wales, Wales World Cup Squad 1975 (captain), British Lions RU, Wales RU
Club honours: Rugby League Championship 1973/74 and 1975/76, Lancashire Cup 1972, BBC2 Floodlit Cup 1974/75

Salford broke the bank when, in October 1967, Brian Snape signed away a reported £16,000 to snare Rugby Union's dazzling star, David Watkins. Watkins said 'I did not know before signing where Salford was and my first introduction to both the city and the football club was on that cold damp evening in October against Oldham. I travelled to the ground with chairman Brian Snape and we were both very nervous. Mr Snape's nervousness was whether his new signing would justify the outlay. Mine was similar – would I prove to be worth the confidence Mr Snape had in my ability?'

Watkins had played for the famous Newport club 202 times, becoming captain in 1964, when he was twenty-two, and was a member of the team to inflict the only defeat on the 1963 All Blacks. His debut for Wales was at Cardiff Arms Park against England in January 1963, and he won 21 caps, being captain on three occasions. With Wales, he enjoyed Five Nations championship glory in 1964, 1965 and 1966. Selected for the British Lions tour to Australia and New Zealand in 1966, he played in two Tests against Australia and four – two as captain – against New Zealand.

In only his second season at Salford, he took over the captaincy and led them to Wembley. Although leaving disappointed, he gained consolation by leading the side to the 1972 Lancashire Cup and 1973/74 championship successes. The captaincy transferred to Chris Hesketh in 1974, but Watkins gave full support, helping to capture the championship for the second time in three seasons in 1975/76, and was on hand to set up Keith Fielding's crucial try in the dramatic Floodlit Cup final replay victory at Warrington in 1975. He played in the finals of the Lancashire Cup (1973 and 1975), the Players Trophy (1973) and the Premiership (1976) but had to settle for runners-up medals. He missed the 1974 Lancashire Cup final defeat due to his short-lived retirement.

If there was a challenge for Watkins in Rugby League, it was adapting to the role of stand-off and, after 123 matches, coach Cliff Evans switched him to the centre in a controversial but inspired move. As Watkins himself said: 'In Union, I made my name at stand-off, but it was not my best position in League. It didn't suit my style. When I switched to centre I had more room in which to work.' Watkins never really looked back from that point, his pace being seen to devastating effect, and in 1971/72 he logged 30 tries, the highest return ever in a season from a Salford centre. His three tries in five minutes in ⁀ecember 1972, against Barrow, made it into the *Guinness Book of Records*!

In April 1970, Maurice Richards, who had taken on the goal-kicking duties, cried off a match with Batley due to a broken nose. Watkins stood in and kicked four goals. 'I had never done any goal kicking before apart from a bit in junior football' he said. In the next three seasons, he blasted Salford's kicking and point scoring records out of sight, creating a new high each time. In 1972/73, he set a world record of 221 goals, failing by just three points to equal Lewis Jones' all-time points record of 496. He matched Gus Risman's record of 13 goals in a match, against Keighley in January 1972. From April 1971 to April 1974, he played a Rugby League record 140 consecutive matches (overtaken by Keith Elwell of Widnes in 1982) and scored in 92 successive games during that run (still a Rugby League record).

A first international appearance came when he represented Wales against England at The Willows in November 1968, the first of sixteen matches for his native land, and he was captain of Wales' World Cup party to Australia and New Zealand in 1975. He coached them in 1976/77 (partnering Bill Francis), and independently from 1982 to 1985. March 1971 marked his Great Britain debut against France and he was a member of the 1974 tour squad. He made six appearances for Great Britain and was coach to the 1977 British World Cup party to the Antipodes.

The 1974 tour almost resulted in the end of his career. In the first match of the New Zealand section, he tore his knee ligaments, having tried to recover from a similar injury sustained earlier in Brisbane, Australia. No one realised he had a fracture above the knee until he returned to Britain. He recovered, resuming with Salford in the match with Keighley on 2 October 1974. Having proved his fitness, he shocked everyone by retiring. He explained later: 'I couldn't afford to pass up becoming

Ours at last! David Watkins in 1972 after leading Salford to their first Lancashire Cup win since 1936 and the club's first major trophy since 1939.

branch manager of the financial firm I worked for at Merthyr Tydfil. Three months later Brian Snape rang me to say the club had injury problems and asked me to help out'. He was persuaded to return in the match with Wakefield on 10 January 1975 and, when Paul Charlton returned to Workington at the end of the season, he had a new role at full-back.

During 1978, he shared a £12,600 testimonial with Hesketh and was awarded an honorary Master of Arts degree by the University of Salford. He finally retired after the match with Rochdale Hornets on 1 April 1979, but came out of retirement to play twenty matches for Swinton in 1979/80. He was managing director for the new Cardiff City RFL club, based at Ninian Park, from 1981, taking over as coach in October of 1981 and continuing until the demise of Cardiff at the end of 1983/84. Watkins even played for Cardiff three times during the 1982/83 season. He was awarded the MBE in the 1986 New Year's honours list.

W. (Billy) Watkins

Scrum-half, 1931-1945

Birthplace: Abertillery
Signed from: Cross Keys RU

Debut: 29 August 1931 v. Oldham (home)
Final match: 22 December 1945 v. Broughton Rangers (away)

Appearances: 360
Tries: 45
Goals: 8
Points: 151

Representative honours: Tourist 1936, Great Britain, Wales, Glamorgan RU
Club honours: Rugby League Championship 1932/33, 1936/37 and 1938/39, Rugby League Challenge Cup 1938, Lancashire Cup 1931, 1934, 1935 and 1936, Lancashire League Championship 1932/33, 1933/34, 1934/35, 1936/37 and 1938/39

When William Edward Watkins – idolised at Salford as 'Billy' – broke his left leg during the 1925/26 season, he was told he would never play again. Within three years, the determined little Welshman had proved the experts wrong and, in 1929, he played in a Welsh Rugby Union trial. He failed to get into the international side but did establish himself in the Glamorgan county side. In the winter of 1930/31, Salford manager Lance Todd saw him playing for Glamorgan against Worcestershire. Todd said: 'I went across to Worcester to watch, and was on the scent of another half-back when I came across Watkins. I think I was the only spectator there. Watkins took a long time for me to land but, as the other player also came north to join another club without breaking any ice, I think I can call it a lucky change over.'

It was during the summer of 1931 that Todd made his bid. Watkins said: 'I told him I wanted to try for my Welsh cap. He extracted a promise from me that I would not sign for anyone else. He was persistent, however, and the next time he called he said "what if you break your leg again? I won't want you and nobody else will!" This was his craftiness! He made me waver and I changed my mind. He offered me £350. I had never seen £350 in my life. He put his hand inside his pocket and pulled out a huge wad of notes. There must have been £1,000. I was flabbergasted. He said "If you sign I will give your mum £50 as well". She said "I don't want to sell you!" but Todd had convinced me and, in June 1931, I joined Salford'.

He was paired with Reggie Meek for his first match and the following week he was teamed up with Emlyn Jenkins for the first time, although it was during the following season that they became a regular partnership. Within three months of making his debut, he was in the Lancashire Cup final against Swinton, the Reds winning 10-8. The out-half was Meek, Jenkins playing on the left wing. After the Jenkins-Watkins combination became established, everything revolved around their brilliant, almost telepathic, pairing. Together they played in the championship finals of 1933, 1934 and 1937 and the Lancashire Cup finals in 1934, 1935 and 1936. With the exception of the 1934 championship final, all ended in victory. The inseparable pair made their Great Britain debuts together in the Third Test at Swinton

Billy Watkins, far left, brings the ball away from the scrum in a match against Wakefield Trinity at The Willows in March 1938.

in December 1933. Britain won 19-16 and a report said: 'The association of Watkins and Jenkins at half back was a triumph. The scrum-half (Watkins) played the game of his life.'

Watkins won a place on the 1936 tour, and played in the final two Tests against Australia and both matches against New Zealand. He had his final two Test appearances in the series against the 1937 Kangaroos. In each of his seven Test matches, he had combined with Jenkins. His first representative match in Rugby League was at Salford in January 1932 when he played for Wales against England. He appeared six times for the Welsh side, winning the European Championship in 1935/36.

A profile of Watkins in the 1930s said: 'He is stockily built, but as strong as an ox. The manner in which he will go down to stop an opponent's forward rush is amazing and he is as good as a seventh forward on such occasions. Watkins is not orthodox, he fashions his play on the situation as it arises and, being a quick thinker, opponents are at a loss to know what he will do next.' Following the departure of Jenkins early in 1938, Watkins continued to enjoy success at Salford. The biggest day of his career was at Wembley for the 1938 Challenge Cup win over Barrow. Gus Risman was at stand-off, and the two played together again in the unsuccessful Lancashire Cup final bid later that year. Returning to Wembley in 1939, Watkins was paired with newcomer Tom Kenny. That final was lost but they shared in the Championship final win over Castleford the following weekend.

After the Second World War, Watkins played just seven matches for Salford before transferring to Belle Vue Rangers in August 1946. As with Salford, he found himself in a Lancashire Cup final within months of signing, but the Rangers lost to Wigan, as they did again in the 1947 final. In the former he was reunited with Kenny, whilst his partner in 1947 was ex-Abertillery half-back Ray Price, destined for fame with Warrington and Great Britain. Watkins played 87 times for Belle Vue, the last being in September 1948.

Stuart Whitehead

Second row forward/centre three-quarter, 1966-1972

Birthplace: Oldham
Signed from: Oldham

Debut: 17 September 1966 v. Workington Town (away)
Final match: 21 October 1972 v. Swinton (at Warrington)

Appearances: 223 (includes 20 as substitute)
Tries: 56
Goals: 0
Points: 168

Representative honours: Lancashire
Club honours: Lancashire Cup 1972, Second Division Championship 1963/64 (Oldham)

Referring to Salford's 1969 Challenge Cup semi-final victory over Warrington at Wigan's Central Park, David Watkins said: 'The star was Stuart Whitehead. He came into Rugby League as a hard, rugged second row forward. When Salford bought Colin Dixon and Mike Coulman, he switched to the centre and it was his battering runs through the middle that brought him a try, and paved the way for two more by Paul Jackson and Bill Burgess.' For Whitehead, it was a match where he had been determined to put to bed the spectre of 1964 when, playing for Oldham, he had gone out in the second replay of the semi-final to Hull Kingston Rovers. He had signed for Oldham in 1961 from Shawcross Juniors and helped them take the Second Division title – and promotion – in that memorable 1963/64 campaign before joining the Reds for £2,000 in 1966.

He made his Salford debut at Workington Town in September 1966 playing in the second row, and soon had the fans behind him as he began to use his bulk to power through opposing defences. His pace in the back row made him the club's top try scorer in 1967/68, when he recorded 16 touchdowns. As mentioned by Watkins, competition for the second row increased and with Welshman Ron Hill also arriving via Castleford, Whitehead transferred to the three-quarters with great success, becoming a key component in the machine that took the Reds to Wembley that year.

He reverted to the pack in 1970, where he continued to be a valuable member of the squad. Almost ironically, his one major honour with Salford was accomplished in his final match for the club. That was the 1972 Lancashire Cup final against Swinton, where he formed a useful back row partnership with Dixon and Eric Prescott as the Reds completed a 25-11 victory. Just two weeks later, he was making his first appearance in Rochdale Hornets colours and, in 1974, he was in their Players Trophy final line-up, where he played at prop in the 27-16 defeat by Warrington. He continued to play for the Hornets until 1976. He did not receive the recognition that most experts believed he should have had, making just two county appearances – for Lancashire against the Australians at Salford in October 1967 and in opposition to Yorkshire at Craven Park, Hull during September 1968.

Jack Williams

Forward, 1897-1906

Birthplace: St Thomas, near Swansea
Signed from: Swansea RU

Debut: 4 September 1897 v. St Helens (home)
Final match: 17 November 1906 v. Leigh (home)

Appearances: 269
Tries: 9
Goals: 0
Points: 27

Representative honours: Lancashire, Glamorgan RU
Club honours: none

Former Swansea Rugby Union powerhouse Jack Williams took just six competitive matches in Salford colours before the Lancashire selectors got their clutches into him and persuaded him he was a Lancastrian! He had first appeared for the Reds after the 1896/97 campaign had concluded, signing in April 1897 aged twenty, and playing in five end-of-season friendly games, his first being on 10 April at home to Wakefield Trinity. Williams had played Rugby Union for Danygraig at sixteen and then Swansea when they took over that club. At nineteen, he represented Glamorgan county and a year later he was picked for Wales. However, the match, against Scotland, was cancelled owing to a dispute.

His impact on the Salford team in 1897/98 was instantaneous and Lancashire soon took notice, offering him a place in the county trial match just one month and two days after his official club debut. His appearance in Lancashire's pack to meet Cheshire at Oldham on 16 October meant he had to miss Salford's match at Rochdale Hornets, the first of two he missed for Salford that season. The second absence was when the club rested him for the fixture with Leigh on 8 April 1898 because they were playing in the Challenge Cup semi-final the next day! The gesture was in vain, as Batley won 5-0 on their way to retaining the cup.

Williams, whose first season with Salford coincided with the arrival of Jack Rhapps and Pat Tunney as the club recruited a tougher 'breed' of forward, did appear in three Challenge Cup finals for Salford, however. In 1900, 1902 and 1903 they reached the big day but Williams had to share the ignominy of defeat in each one, in addition to the loss to Bradford in the 1904 championship decider.

He added to his Lancashire tally by representing the county three more times during 1898 – including the match with Yorkshire at Salford's New Barnes enclosure in November – and twice in 1899, his final appearance being against Cheshire at Swinton's Chorley Road ground in November. On New Year's Day 1906, he broke his leg against Leigh which kept him out until September that year, and this effectively ended his career. He managed six appearances at the start of 1906/07, the club officially announcing his retirement in August 1907.

Peter Williams
Centre three-quarter, 1988-1994

Birthplace: Wigan
Signed from: Orrell RU

Debut: 23 March 1988 v. Leigh (home)
Final match: 24 April 1994 v. Featherstone Rovers (away)

Appearances: 154 (includes 8 as substitute)
Tries: 35
Goals: 0
Points: 140

Representative honours: Great Britain, Wales, Lancashire, England RU, Lancashire RU
Club honours: Second Division Championship 1990/91, Second Division Premiership 1991

Peter Nicholas Williams made a quick impact at The Willows, after signing for a reported £50,000 five-year contract in March 1988, one hour after he had, apparently, been named for the England Rugby Union tour Down Under. After three matches for Salford, he was included in the stand-by squad for Great Britain's 1988 tour of Australasia. He did not make the trip but was to play for Britain twice the following year against France at Wigan and Avignon.

Williams proved one of chairman John Wilkinson's most exciting captures from Rugby Union, ending a pursuit by Salford that had taken several years. The former Orrell stand-off had made four appearances for England Rugby Union in 1987 and represented Lancashire on sixteen occasions. In Rugby League, the six-footer found his best position to be in the centre. He was to prove the perfect all-round player. His classy centre play, general alertness and his touch-finding were a revelation from a player who had spent most of his playing career outside of Rugby League. He became team captain in 1988/89 and continued in that role for two seasons. In October 1988, he had his first big date with Salford when they reached the final of the Lancashire Cup, going down after a tough fight against Wigan 22-17 at St Helens. Williams, as captain, was at full-back through Steve Gibson's suspension. His substitution in the sixty-eighth minute due to being concussed turned the game away from Salford.

In 1990, he was back in the Lancashire Cup final with Salford, but his early try was not enough to prevent the Reds losing to Widnes 24-18. That 1990/91 season finished on a high, however, as Salford walked away with the Second Division title and won the Premiership final at Old Trafford against Halifax. Williams missed that final through injury, but had played a critical part – unusually at stand-off – in winning the semi-final replay at Workington Town.

He played in the 1989 'War of the Roses' match for Lancashire against Yorkshire and in December 1992 he represented Wales against France at Wigan, qualifying through his father Roy, a former Llanelli forward who had joined Wigan in the 1950s. He was chosen again by Wales to face New Zealand in October 1993 at Swansea, but never left the dug-out.

Sam Williams

Forward/three-quarter, 1881-1890

Birthplace: Salford
Signed from: Swinton

Debut: 8 October 1881 v. Manchester Athletic (away)
Final match: 26 April 1890 v. Wigan (home)

Appearances: 170
Tries: 27
Goals: 2

Representative honours: Tourist (RU) 1888, North of England RU, Lancashire RU
Club honours: none

Samuel Williams was one of the mainstays of Salford during the glorious decade of the 1880s, when the club dominated the Lancashire rugby scene. He was another product of the Salford-based Crescent side, turning out amongst the forwards from 1879. When they merged with Salford in 1881, he joined Swinton, playing for their reserves but later decided to reunite with his former colleagues at Salford. He made his debut in the pack at Manchester Athletic in the third match of 1881/82 but, unable to command a regular first team place, played just four times that season, all in the three-quarters.

In 1882/83, he did not miss a game, scoring 8 tries (making him the club's top try scorer) and 2 drop goals, in a campaign where only three matches were lost. His performance in the last match of the season against Bolton was described as 'being one of the very finest ever seen on any ground'. Reputed to be a true gentleman, throughout 1884/85 he voluntarily played as captain of the reserve side, to assist the development of some of the club's younger players.

In October 1885, he returned to the forwards for a home match against Oldham and never looked back, creating a reputation as a forward with an appetite for work. He was voted first team-captain in 1887/88, an honour that was repeated for 1889/90. In March 1889, he represented Salford in the match against the touring Maori team.

On the 8 November 1886, he took his first steps towards wider recognition when invited to take part in the Lancashire county trial at Whalley Range, representing South Lancashire against North Lancashire. He caught the selectors' eyes and was included for his debut against Cheshire at Birkenhead Park the following week. That season, he played four times for the county, although he was not to represent them again in the future. Having broken into the Lancashire side, his next big moment was on 18 December 1886 when he played in the annual North of England versus South of England match at Blackheath. He was the first of three Salford players to appear in this annual challenge, viewed at the time as being one stage lower than full England selection although, unfortunately, that did not transpire in Williams' case. In 1888, he joined Jack Anderton, Harry Eagles and Tom Kent on the first ever rugby tour to Australia and New Zealand, playing in 50 of the 52 matches, a figure surpassed only by Eagles.

Stewart Williams

Loose forward/second row forward/centre three-quarter, 1977-1984

Birthplace: Salford
Signed from: Salford Colts ARL

Debut: 6 December 1977 substitute v. St Helens (away)
Final match: 23 December 1984 v. Sheffield Eagles (home)

Appearances: 223 (includes 40 as substitute)
Tries: 60
Goals: 0
Points: 197

Representative honours: none
Club honours: none

In 1980/81, Salford coach Alex Murphy was grooming Stewart Williams as loose forward successor to Eric Prescott, by moving Prescott into the second row. Having missed only three matches in 1979/80, Williams' pace and keen tackling had already won him recognition with a place in the Lancashire shadow squad and Murphy commented: 'It will do a lot for his confidence. It means he knows other people are noticing him and not just ourselves.'

He first played for the Eccles Rugby Union club for six months as a centre, moving to Rugby League with Langworthy Juniors. He then joined Salford Colts, and was coached by Ivor Edwards and Dai Moses. 'It was a happy time, we had some good trips and Ivor and Dai gave me a lot of encouragement' he said. It was whilst playing for the Colts that he moved into the pack. 'We were short of forwards so I said I'd have a go and that's how I ended up in the second row'. He signed as a professional for Salford in April 1977, making his first appearance as a substitute at St Helens in a narrow 7-4 floodlit cup semi-final defeat on 6 December 1977. That was followed by a try-scoring full debut in the second row at Widnes a few weeks later, on Boxing Day.

By 1978/79, he commanded a regular back-row spot and, with the transfer of Prescott to Widnes, took over as loose-forward during 1980/81. A further change of position came about, however, when his combined strength and speed was put to use in the centre, where he first appeared in January 1982. One report said: 'Williams' progress since moving into the backs has been encouraging and he could well be on the verge of an exciting new chapter in his career'. That view was confirmed when, following a home Lancashire Cup-tie with Fulham in September 1983, a match report exclaimed: 'Stewart Williams was the toast of Salford last night. His 70-yard touchdown, two minutes from time, earned Salford a breathtaking Lancashire Cup victory. As time ticked away, Gerard Byrne broke clear to send Williams racing in between the sticks for a last gasp try.'

In September 1985 he was transferred to Barrow, following a period on loan to Wigan, and later played for Chorley Borough, during the 1989/90 campaign. In just over four seasons with Barrow, he played 115 times, registering 27 tries in 1985/86. He made just three appearances for Wigan and 16 for Chorley.

Syd Williams
Wing three-quarter/full-back, 1939-1952

Birthplace: Aberavon
Signed from: Aberavon RU

Debut: 14 October 1939 v. Broughton Rangers (home)
Final match: 20 September 1952 v. Dewsbury (away)

Appearances: 222
Tries: 81
Goals: 43
Points: 329

Representative honours: Wales, Wales RU
Club honours: none

The Rugby League career of Sydney Arthur Williams got off to a bad start in more than one way. Reputed to be the best winger in Welsh Rugby Union, the twenty-year-old signed for Salford just after the 1938/39 season had finished. He had played three times for Wales in their 1939 championship season and represented the Barbarians. The first glimpse the Salford fans had of him was in the public trial matches that heralded the ill-fated 1939/40 season. An initial setback came when a fractured wrist in one of the trials gave him the worst possible start. He was unable to make his first appearance until mid-October – a two-try debut against Broughton Rangers – but by that time, the second blow to his professional career had already landed! Three games into the season, the Second World War was declared and sport was in turmoil.

On the playing front, Williams managed 12 tries from 23 matches in that sombre first season, playing mostly in the centre and creating a good impression, one pundit writing: 'I shall be greatly surprised if he does not prove to be one of the best centres who has ever donned the Salford jersey. His power, speed and ability to swerve in either direction are ideal assets.' He played in all 14 matches during 1940/41, scoring 14 tries – four of them in one match with Liverpool Stanley – as the season ended prematurely, Salford 'shutting up shop' after their Christmas Day match with Wigan.

Due to his country's call, he made just four appearances for Salford in the first post-war season of 1945/46, but was available from the next campaign, returning to his more accustomed wing slot, his modest tally of 11 tries topping the club's list. From 1949, he became the regular full-back until his retirement; the exception was the 1950/51 campaign when Glyn Moses provided the last line of defence, Williams being out injured for much of that term. Williams had been seriously hurt in the Easter Monday clash with Wigan in April 1950 and there was real doubt about him coming back. One writer described his return to action in January 1951 as 'amazing'.

Williams played in two Rugby League internationals for Wales against England during the Second World War (in 1940 and 1943), adding a further three appearances in peacetime. He played twice more against England (1947 and 1952) and against Other Nationalities at Abertillery in 1949.

Tom Williams

Centre three-quarter, 1897-1902

Birthplace: Penrhillfer, Glamorgan
Signed from: Llwynpia RU (Pontypridd)

Debut: 4 September 1897 v. St Helens (home)
Final match: 18 October 1902 v. Broughton Rangers (home)

Appearances: 140
Tries: 84
Goals: 14
Points: 280

Representative honours: Lancashire, Glamorgan RU
Club honours: none

Thomas Williams, described as 'one of the most brilliant three-quarter backs ever seen on a football field', was the first Welshman to lead a Challenge Cup final team when he did so with Salford against Swinton in 1900. Previously captain of the Llwynpia club, he began a tradition at Salford for great Welsh skippers – which would include Willie Thomas, Jack Gore, Billy Williams, Gus Risman, Alan Edwards, Dai Davies, David Watkins and latterly David Young. Williams was the Reds' leader from 1898 until 1902 and in charge for the first match played at The Willows in December 1901. Before joining the Reds, he had been first reserve for the Welsh Rugby Union side in 1896/97.

At Salford, he soon made a name for himself, scoring a club record 29 tries in his first campaign. His 107 points, with the help of 10 goals, was also a club record. Williams' prolific partnership with wingman Joe Hoskins was the talk of the league, Hoskins himself scoring 28 for Salford. Their 57-try spectacular had one expert saying: 'Williams and Hoskins are now as fine a right wing pair as can be desired – a wing that seems irresistible at times'. Williams and Hoskins were also the leading scorers in the Northern Union, Hoskins finishing ahead of his skipper courtesy of two additional tries with Lancashire. In 1902, Williams led his troops to another Challenge Cup final but Broughton Rangers ruined the day with an emphatic 25-0 win, making it two defeats from two finals. His worst day as skipper was when five of his side was dismissed in the 1899 semi-final with Hunslet.

By the end of his first season, he had impressed the selectors sufficiently to be included in the Lancashire side to meet Westmoreland in March 1898, at Broughton Rangers' Wheaters' Field ground. He made 6 appearances for the county, the last being in December 1900 against Cheshire at Stockport. Tragically, his career was curtailed when, with 25 minutes left to play, he injured his left knee making a tackle in a match with Broughton Rangers on 18 October 1902. Carried from the field, he never played for Salford again. In August 1904, it was reported that, although he had returned to live in Llwynpia, he had put in a transfer request with Salford; but, apparently, he did not play again.

W.A. (Billy) Williams

Prop forward, 1927-1938

Birthplace: Crumlin, Monmouthshire
Signed from: Crumlin RU

Debut: 15 October 1927 v. St Helens (away)
Final match: 1 October 1938 v. Hull (away)

Appearances: 435
Tries: 14
Goals: 0
Points: 42

Representative honours: Tourist 1928 and 1932, Great Britain, Wales, Other Nationalities, Glamorgan & Monmouthshire, Wales RU
Club honours: Rugby League Championship 1932/33 and 1936/37, Rugby League Challenge Cup 1938, Lancashire Cup 1931, 1934, 1935 and 1936, Lancashire League Championship 1932/33, 1933/34, 1934/35 and 1936/37

William Arthur Williams – known as 'Billy' – was the first Salford skipper since Willie Thomas in 1914 to lift silverware. The Lancashire Cup was finally landed in October 1931, followed less than two years later by an even bigger prize – the Rugby League Championship trophy. Williams was twenty-one when he signed up with Salford for £250 in 1927 (the same year his brother Llewellyn also joined the Reds) and swiftly developed into a powerful open side prop forward. Another product of Welsh Rugby Union, he spent three years with Cross Keys and two with Crumlin, representing Wales four times during 1927. He took over the captaincy of Salford from Alf Middleton in September 1931 and continued to lead the side until 1935, when he handed the responsibility on to Gus Risman.

Williams caught the eye of the tour committee only four months into his Rugby League career and was included in the trial match at the Athletic Grounds, Rochdale in February 1928. He passed the test and, after only one season in the game, was on the boat for the 1928 trip to Australia and New Zealand. Although he did not play in any of the Tests, he appeared in 12 of the tour matches. In 1930, he made his debut with three international sides: Great Britain in the fourth Test against Australia at Rochdale on 15 January, Wales three days later against the same opposition at Wembley, and Other Nationalities (for the only time) against England at St Helens in December. In 1932, he toured again, playing his only other Test match, the third against Australia in Sydney. He played twice more for Wales, against England at The Willows in 1932 and against Australia in 1933 – again at Wembley – and represented Glamorgan and Monmouthshire five times from 1929 until 1931.

He enjoyed considerable success at Salford, adding the 1936/37 championship and the 1934, 1935 and 1936 Lancashire Cups to his earlier triumphs. He was also the losing captain in the 1933/34 championship final. In 1937/38 – his last full season before retiring – he celebrated his greatest moment, playing in the team that won the 1938 Challenge Cup at Wembley, providing a perfect end to a glittering career in what was his testimonial year. He later joined the Salford board.

Ernie Woods

Forward, 1914-1925

Birthplace: Salford
Signed from: Weaste ARL

Debut: 10 January 1914 v. Oldham (home)
Final match: 3 January 1925 v. Leigh (home)

Appearances: 230 (includes 44 in wartime)
Tries: 13 (includes 4 in wartime)
Goals: 0
Points: 39 (includes 12 in wartime)

Representative honours: none
Club honours: Rugby League Championship 1913/14

Ernest Woods was the classic case of the local boy makes good, taking his place in the Salford pack for the Championship final victory over Huddersfield in 1914, just months after his first appearance in the side. He was, at 5 ft 11 in and over 13 stone, a big, strong forward for that period and his debut, coming as it did in January 1914, was timed perfectly from his point of view. Signed in October 1913, he had taken over from George Thom in the forwards during a season when the club used surprisingly few players in the first team – just twenty-two. The consistent line-up contributed to the Reds taking second place in the championship table. Woods more than held his own with the more established members of the side, earning good reviews in the press for his exploits, particularly his solid defence.

His appearance in the play-offs had an impact at the semi-final stage when, playing the biggest game of his relatively short career, he pushed over for a try as Salford put out Wigan 16-5 to earn a place against Huddersfield. In the final, he played his part in a pack that denied the Yorkshire team possession, thwarting any second-half recovery after Salford led 5-3 at the interval.

One of three Salfordians in the team, it was also reported that 'Woods stood out in attack'.

There was, unfortunately, only one full season left before serious competition was put on hold due to the First World War. In 1914/15, he was one of the thirteen Salford players suspended 'en bloc' by the Northern Union throughout January for not agreeing to make deductions in their match fees for the 'Relief Fund'. Although that was eventually resolved, all competitive fixtures were soon placed on hold until peace resumed, clubs arranging friendly games from the 1915/16 season. Woods continued to turn out for Salford until the early months of 1917, when he was required for the war effort.

Once the war was over, he returned to The Willows, playing in four friendly matches during November and December 1918, prior to competitive rugby starting again in January 1919. There would be no more medals, the Salford side of the post-First World War period being a shadow of the 1914 champions, but he continued to play regularly and was a popular clubman up to his final 1924/25 season.